# Preventing Corporate Embezzlement

# Preventing Corporate Embezzlement

**Paul Shaw**

**Jack Bologna**

BUTTERWORTH
HEINEMANN

Boston    Oxford    Aukland    Johannesburg    Melbourne    New Delhi

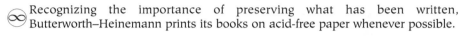
**Library of Congress Cataloging-in-Publication Data**

Shaw, Paul (Paul D.)

    Preventing corporate embezzlement/Paul Shaw, Jack Bologna.
     p. cm.
    Includes bibliographical references and index.
    ISBN 0-7506-7254-4 (pbk. :alk. paper)
     1. Commercial crimes—Prevention. 2. Embezzlement—Prevention.
    3. Employee theft—Prevention. 4. Employee crimes—Prevention.
    I. Bologna, Jack. II. Title

    HF5549.5.E43 S5 2000
    658.4′73—dc21

                               99-089139

**British Library Cataloguing-in-Publication Data**
A catalogue record for this book is available from the British Library.

The publisher offers special discounts on bulk orders of this book.

For information, please contact:

Manager of Special Sales
Butterworth-Heinemann
225 Wildwood Avenue
Woburn, MA 01801-2041
Tel: 781-904-2500
Fax: 781-904-2620

For information on all Butterworth–Heinemann publications available, contact our World Wide Web home page at: http://www.focalpress.com

10 9 8 7 6 5 4 3 2 1

Printed in the United States of America

# Contents

# Preface

Next to internal theft, embezzlement is the most common crime against businesses and other organizations. It is estimated that embezzlers steal $4 to $6 billion a year from their employers in stores, credit unions, law firms, banks, hospitals, churches, and schools. No organization of any size is immune.

Unfortunately, thefts by embezzlers are rarely detected; if detected, their crimes are seldom prosecuted, and if prosecuted, their sentences are usually very light. And many victims decide to settle out of court to avoid embarrassing publicity.

Embezzlers often hold positions of trust in a company, which means they have ready access to books, records, cash, and other assets. Computers offer embezzlers with some computing and accounting skills a new and easy way to steal and to make their crime harder to detect and prosecute.

Employers enhance the opportunity for embezzlement by having most or all financial operations on the computer, putting one person in charge, and having lax internal financial controls or none at all. All an embezzler needs is control of the computer or one or more of its financial operations, such as payroll or accounts payable.

Most owners and managers have only a vague idea of the extent of workplace crime and how embezzlements are carried out. Too often there is owner or management disbelief that the company could become a victim of fraud, theft, or embezzlement. Almost all fraud and embezzlements have occurred because specific controls were compromised, either intentionally or accidentally, or their warnings were ignored by management.

*Preventing Corporate Embezzlement* starts from the premise that a vital management responsibility is the protection of the organization's assets. This book argues that controls and security can reduce the opportunity for workplace theft, fraud, and embezzlement, and that these controls must be monitored and enforced.

Managers, auditors, security personnel, risk managers, and others charged with protecting assets must achieve a heightened awareness of embezzlement, recognize and understand the opportunities, means, methods, and varieties of embezzlement, and establish and monitor internal controls that will prevent and detect embezzlement.

In addition to internal controls, employers must do preemployment checks; learn to recognize activities and behavior of employees that could indicate possible theft; distribute an antitheft policy to employees; bond employees in fiduciary positions; get crime insurance; and conduct surprise fraud-focused audits in addition to thorough audits of a company's financial controls.

*Preventing Corporate Embezzlement* gives comprehensive yet concise analyses of:

- Embezzler motives, opportunities, and methods; how to recognize "red flags" of embezzlement.

- The law relating to theft, fraud, and embezzlement, as well as conspiracy, money laundering, internal investigations, and the liability that can attach to the company and its owner/managers from not taking steps to deter and detect fraud, embezzlement, and theft.

- How to fashion workplace theft policies and codes of conduct (sample policies are provided), along with ways to communicate compliance to employees.

- How to establish cost-effective internal protection controls, including the use of employee preemployment screening, physical security measures, and specific controls to protect financial assets.

- How to conduct audits of policies, codes of conduct, internal protection controls, and security systems; extensive audit and security checklists are provided.

- How to conduct a thorough investigation of a possible embezzlement, who should guide the investigation, and the investigative team members.

- How to manage embezzlement and theft risks with employee dishonesty insurance and fidelity bonding; when to provide notice of loss and how to investigate and recover for losses.

*Preventing Corporate Embezzlement* includes a unique communication and training package to enhance the effectiveness of an organization's compliance program. The book's eight "Think Like a Thief" scenarios found in Chapter 18 test and reinforce awareness of weaknesses in internal controls and specific vulnerabilities to embezzlement, theft, and fraud.

Also included is an easily administered training program with a leader's guide and a participant evaluation form, plus a script and a set of 24 presentations that can be used as overheads in creating a company-specific fraud and embezzlement awareness program. The book also includes a listing of publications and other sources of information on embezzlement, internal controls and security, auditing, and insurance.

# Embezzlement: Would You Know One if You Saw One?

Embezzlers steal $4 to $6 billion a year from their employers, masters, and principals. Yet their thefts are rarely detected. Even when detected, their crimes are rarely prosecuted, and if embezzlers are prosecuted, their criminal sentences are very light. How do we prevent embezzlement? Indeed, how do we even detect embezzlement?

The crime of embezzlement generally consists of the fraudulent misappropriation of the property of an employer, principal, or master by an employee, agent, or servant to whom possession of that property has been entrusted. Typically, embezzlement occurs when an employee, agent, or servant gains initial possession of property lawfully, but subsequently misappropriates it. In this respect, embezzlement is different from larceny (theft). Larceny is committed when property is taken without the owner's consent.

## Who Are All These People With Sticky Fingers?_____

And what makes them behave the way they do? The classic definition of an embezzler in the literature of criminology is someone who holds a position of trust and finds himself with an unspeakable problem, usually of a financial nature, that can be resolved by "borrowing" the funds of his employer. (Borrowing usually is a rationalization.) There are a few other characteristics as well. Embezzlers tend to have low self-esteem or a compulsive personality that may manifest itself in gambling, drinking or eating excessively, and in the pursuit of an expensive lifestyle or hobbies or both. They are also said to generally commit their acts of defalcation alone, over extended periods of time, and in increasing amounts before they are apprehended. Yet there is no common, scientifically identifiable set of characteristics, personality traits, or personal problems that distinguishes embezzlers.

## The Embezzler's Motives

Motives for embezzlement or theft are traditionally categorized as:

1. Economic. This motive reflects on the part of the embezzler either a need or greed.
2. Egotistic. Showing off—proving that one can beat the system or compromise the control—is an egotistic motive.
3. Ideological. Ideological motives stem from a perceived need by the embezzler for revenge, because the organization targeted by the theft is considered to have harmed in some fashion either the embezzler or some other individual.
4. Psychotic. Some form of obsessive-compulsive behavior prompts the embezzler to steal or to engage in some form of activity that is understood to be prohibited.

A given embezzler may have one or more of these motives. The most common reason for embezzling seems simply to be greed.

## Where the Embezzler Operates

Embezzlers usually hold positions of trust in a company, which means they have ready access to books, records, cash, and other assets. Long-term, trusted employees are often very familiar with the controls and safeguards and are able to exploit whatever weaknesses exist. Embezzlers are adept at finding a company's control weaknesses or making "patches" in computer programs to facilitate or hide a theft trail. While each embezzler has a pattern of theft that is somewhat unique, embezzlers generally commit their thefts alone, over a long period of time taking increasing amounts.

### Government Programs and Nonprofits Often Easy Targets

Embezzlers working in the public sector often find easy pickings for theft. Here are a few real cases:

1. A bookkeeper for a city board is able to embezzle over $80,000; auditors say the bookkeeping system was a shambles, basic auditing controls were not in place; receipts and other documentation were missing. The bookkeeper cut herself extra paychecks and forged the director's signature on reimbursement checks for payments on her personal credit card, as well as on checks for cash.
2. A fire chief and his former secretary forged more than 90 checks totaling over $200,000. The secretary would sign the name of the fire district treasurer, and the fire chief would endorse them, then cash the checks. The two said they had a gambling problem and spent most of the money at casinos. The chief said, "Every cent I had went to the machines."
3. As supervisor of Indiana's child support program, David Scott was paid over $26,000 a year. Prosecutors say that Scott collected far more than that—about $685,000—in an eight-year scheme in which he created phony child support cases to finance sexual relations with four women. Prosecutors say

it is the worst case of embezzlement in state history. Scott, who is a married father of two, was charged with five counts of forgery and one count each of corrupt business influence, theft, computer tampering, and official misconduct. Four women were also arrested in connection with the reported scheme. Scott was one of only three employees with full access to computerized records of 300,000 active child-support cases in the state. The authorities said Scott issued 360 false checks, totaling $684,516, to himself and four female acquaintances starting in January 1991, and then erased the evidence. Part of the money was used to pay off personal debts and to buy a fur coat, a car, and furniture. An exotic dancer used some of the money to buy breast implants, the prosecutor's office said.

4.  A United Way accounting supervisor was indicted for embezzling $63,000 from the agency. Checks were issued for specious building and remodeling projects and then endorsed, cashed, or deposited to accounts created for fictitious contractors.

5.  Over several years a municipal clerk in a small Midwestern town embezzled over $225,000. She supervised the installation of a new computer in which city accounts were kept. She was the only city employee who knew how to operate the tax and water utility applications.

6.  A cashier in a state treasurer's office embezzled $1.15 million. The cashier had access to funds in a state vault and could make entries in the state's accounting journals. When the cash was counted at the time of audit, the cashier made up shortages by replacing missing funds with fictitious checks.

## Embezzlement in Labor Unions

What is it about labor unions that makes them particularly vulnerable to internal fraud? Well, for one thing, high-level union officers who set the moral tone for the union may themselves be corrupt. Their conduct is therefore often imitated by lower-level union officials. For another thing, union accounting systems may not provide adequate internal controls to detect and prevent fraud.

While labor unions are assumed to be vulnerable to internal fraud, there is no hard proof that indicates union officers and employees are more crime-prone than other members of society.

But there is a distinguishing characteristic between union organizations and for-profit organizations. Many nonprofit union organizations have been managed by officers who are related by blood or marriage and have been in the union hierarchy for several generations. They tend to feel they own the union. Its funds, therefore, are their own. They can use them at their will.

1.  Union officers have been found guilty of embezzling as much as $700,00 in a scheme that ran a decade. In another case, a union boss carried out an embezzlement by intentionally overpaying a travel agency for conferences and conventions attended by members. The travel agency would refund the overpayments, and she would retain the excess.

## Embezzlement in Banks

1. A "conspiracy of gentlemen" it was called: In 1929, 15 employees—tellers and officers—of the Union Industrial Bank in Flint, Michigan, embezzled over $3 million. Their goal was to make money in the then booming stock market. Their plan was to use money, "borrowed without approval," from the bank. They planned to repay the money and interest from expected earnings in the stock market. The scam depended mainly on the use of cash deposited with the bank and then placed in the New York call money market where it earned interest. This was a common practice. Customers were given a receipt for their money deposited. The conspirators would recall the money from New York within hours after it got there. Now the money was theirs and available to invest in Wall Street stocks. If a customer wanted his money back, other bank accounts were diverted, and the books properly juggled. The scheme worked for months, but losses increased as the market went mostly down instead of up, and more depositors' money was needed to meet margin calls. Finally, when the market crashed on October 29, 1929, the embezzlers had lost $3,592,000 of the bank's money. The 15 embezzlers confessed to the bank's president. The chairman of the board, financier Charles Stewart Mott, replaced the entire amount stolen using his own money to keep the bank solvent and running. The embezzlers received prison sentences varying from six months to ten years.

2. A bank lending officer embezzled over $8 million from the bank over a three-year period. The "MO" was typical for a lending officer. He created 599 fake loans. As loans came due, he created new loans to pay off the old ones.

## Embezzlers as Trustees, Conservators, and Guardians

Attorneys are often given control over escrow or trust funds and money held for clients. Bar rules usually require a segregation of attorney/client funds to prevent commingling and theft. Court-appointed conservators have a fiduciary duty to protect the money and property of a client in probate. Unfortunately, lax or sometimes absent controls have made embezzlement easy. State laws and bar association rules are beginning to tighten, calling for bonding, training, spot audits, credit and criminal background checks, and requiring attorneys to have proof that client funds are clearly segregated.

1. A court-appointed trustee/attorney of a failed brokerage house was charged with embezzling over $100,000. He substituted counterfeit bank certificates of deposit to cover the transfer of funds from the trust account to his own personal bank account.

## Offices and Small Businesses

In a small organization, the office manager's job is to keep the day-to-day operations running smoothly. The office manager may also be the bookkeeper. So one person may do the billing, run payroll, prepare and sign checks, make out and take the deposit to the bank, and reconcile the monthly statement.

From this embezzlement-ripe environment have come an untold number of cases. Typically, the embezzler is described by coworkers in terms such as:

"She was energetic; she set up an excellent bookkeeping system; we never felt we had to check her work."

"He was a devoted employee, a hard worker who hardly ever took a day off."

"He took over every chore. All of us hated recordkeeping and despised the accounting software—it was too difficult and none of us really understand the computer."

"She was the kind of woman people would go to. She would drop whatever she was doing to help."

# How the Embezzler Operates

Embezzlers attempt to make their fraudulent entries look or appear normal by any control criteria (for example, the amount is within established limits, the entry originator is authorized, account classifications are proper, the place and timing of the transaction are appropriate as are the transacting parties, and the subject matter of the transaction is fitting to the needs of the business). Other embezzlers find clever ways to manipulate weaknesses in the accounting and control systems so that their peculations appear to be within the bounds of the weak standards, policies, procedures, and exceptions criteria. Finally, some embezzlers exploit not just weaknesses in controls, but absences of control. There are probably more embezzlements in environments where controls are absent than where controls are weak.

Implausible entries are what fraud auditors tend to look for, such as entries that seem too high, too low, too frequent, too rare, and too irregular in volume, or those made at odd times, by odd persons, at odd places. But the embezzler knows that, too, so he or she tries to dodge those control devices by creating entries that fit within the exceptions or are "smoke screens" designed to throw auditors off the scent, such as small errors intended to distract auditors from the fraudulent entries.

To cover up their activities, for example, embezzlers typically create misinformation or disinformation, destroy information, suppress information or utilize rationalizations if authenticity or accuracy of an entry is challenged. They dream up stories that can justify their entries and thereby create a form of plausible deniability.

# How Embezzlers Manipulate Accounting Systems

To learn how embezzlements occur, one must first have a basic grasp of accounting systems and where and how they can be manipulated. Each stage of the accounting process is susceptible to manipulation and theft. The employee's position within the company will indicate the stage of the process to which he will have access, the extent of control, and the type and magnitude of the potential theft. The greater the access to accounting records and control over the computer system, the greater the possible embezzlement.

The following section looks first at accounting systems and internal controls, then at the areas with classical procedural loopholes that promote fraud, theft, and embezzlement.

## The Basics of Accounting Systems

Accounting is simply the formalized record keeping of the financial transactions of a business. These financial transactions fall into logical groupings that are referred to as accounts. Accounts fall into five major categories: assets, liabilities, owner's equity, expenses, and income. Depending on the degree of sophistication of the accounting that is done by a particular company, these major categories are further broken down into the actual accounts: capital, sales, office supplies, salaries, raw materials, cash, and so forth.

Each financial transaction that takes place affects at least two of these accounts, increasing one by the same amount the other is decreased so that the net effect is zero. In a simple accounting system for example, the purchase of a typewriter decreases the cash account and increases the office equipment and sales tax accounts; the sale of merchandise will decrease the inventory account and increase either the cash and sales discount accounts or the accounts receivable accounts. Ledgers are used to record each financial transaction as it occurs; summaries of these transactions are transferred to the appropriate accounts at the end of an accounting period, usually monthly. At this time the books are balanced to insure that the accounts "zero balance" in total; that is, that the company's assets are equal to its liabilities plus the owner's equity.

This ritual balancing only ensures that the double-entry bookkeeping has been maintained correctly for an entire accounting period—it does not ensure that the correct accounts have been increased and decreased. Only an audit can insure that a cash sale actually resulted in a decrease to the inventory account and an increase to the cash account.

## Manual Accounting Systems

A manual accounting system requires the handwritten entry of all financial transactions for a business. Source documents are forwarded to the bookkeeper, who logs the transactions into the correct ledgers. Ledgers and accounts must be reconciled and balanced at least monthly. The accuracy and validity of input documents, as well as the correct posting of transactions, are the main controls that can be checked by an auditor.

## Computerized Accounting Systems

Computerized accounting systems deal with large amounts of financial data, trying to replace the function of the bookkeeper in the posting, summing, and crossfooting of accounts. However, source documents are still the main form of input that are usually entered directly into the computer. Ledgers and accounts are now balanced "automatically" by the computer, usually more frequently than just at the end of the month. Again, the accuracy and validity of the source documents plus the correct functioning of the computer programs (the bookkeeper) are the main controls that can be checked by an auditor.

## Similarities Between Systems

The similarities between a manual and a computerized accounting system begin with source documents: the sales tickets, expense records, and invoices of all business operations. In a manual system these are forwarded directly to the book-keeper for entry into the account books. Recognition of various types of trans-actions by the bookkeeper and translation into appropriate accounting entries is necessary to properly update the company's journals and ledgers.

Again, in a computerized system, data could be entered directly into the accounting system from a remote terminal or downloaded or reside in a microcomputer; or, data could be generated by a hand-held computer such as an inventory control system. A computer program takes the place of the bookkeeper and records the accounting data into the account master file. The computer program, of course, must recognize different transaction types and post the information to the appropriate accounts.

A major difference between manual and computerized accounting systems is in the storage of master accounts. Records and summary accounts in a manual system are available in a human readable format, often referred to as the "books." Each indi-vidual account can be scrutinized for content, and entries can be checked against source documents. In the computerized system, the books are stored on electronic storage devices. Deciphering the books, therefore, requires transformation of this data back into human-readable formats.

The final process in any accounting system, manual or computerized, is consoli-dation and summarization of various accounts into financial reports and statements. In a manual system this is accomplished by the bookkeeper using the journals and ledgers that make up the books. In a computerized system, an accounting software program is needed to consolidate and present the bookkeeping information in the format required for financial reports and statements. The logic and processes that the bookkeeper goes through in a manual system to prepare trial balances and working papers are paralleled in the computer program.

## Embezzlement Methods

Cash disbursement embezzlement is the most common fraud in books of account. This generally involves the creation of fake documents and false entries, or both, in some category of expense, for example, purchases or payroll, usually in the form of a phony invoice from a phantom supplier or a faked time card from a phantom employee. The fabricated purchases may be for merchandise, raw materials, repairs, maintenance, janitorial or temporary help, insurance, travel and entertainment, benefits, and so forth. Fabricating the purchase of raw material and merchandise is tough to accomplish because costs of manufacture and sale are closely scrutinized by top management. If the fabricated purchases are for services or supplies rather than merchandise or raw material, the fraud is easier to execute and conceal. These expenses are not monitored as closely as costs of manufacture and sale.

Cash disbursement frauds are very common in small firms with one-person accounting departments or in situations in which separation of duties and audit trails are weak or nonexistent. Computerization of small firms exacerbates the disbursement fraud problem, because small business owners are too trusting of data generated by the computer.

Cash receipts frauds are also common in small businesses. The common classic cash receipts fraud involves the lapping of cash and accounts receivable or both, that is, "borrowing" from today's sales or receipts and replacing them with tomorrow's sales or receipts. In either event, the fraud requires the creation of fake data, fake reports, and/or false entries.

There are several other receipts frauds of note. Skimming is holding out or intercepting some of the proceeds of cash sales before any entry is made of their receipt. This is also called fraud on the front end.

Another form of receivables fraud can be generated by the issuance of fake credits for discounts, refunds, rebates, or returns and allowances. Here, a conspiracy may be required with a customer who shares the proceeds of the fake credit with an insider.

## How Internal Fraud, Theft, and Embezzlement First Surface _____

Information concerning an act of employee embezzlement, fraud, theft, or corruption initially surfaces in one of several ways:

1. From an accounting discrepancy, financial irregularity, questionable transaction, or asset loss detected in the course of a routine internal, external, operational, or compliance audit.
2. From a complaint or allegation of such misconduct made by corporate insiders (for example, the employee's peers, subordinates, or superiors).
3. From a complaint or allegation of such misconduct made by corporate outsiders (suppliers, contractors, customers, competitors, police, security, or regulatory officials, and friends, associates, or relatives of the employee).

When an accounting or financial discrepancy surfaces and is noted by an auditor, that information standing alone rarely makes a prima facie case. Very often all the auditor knows for sure at that time is that an adjusting journal entry may be required or that financial statements may need to be corrected. But the discrepancy should not be allowed to stand without follow-up action. The question, then, is what action should be taken and by whom?

Discrepancies and questionable transactions discovered by auditors should be brought to the immediate attention of higher authorities in audit, general management, legal, and security functions. Complaints or allegations of employee theft, fraud, and the like, received from insiders or outsiders should be brought to the immediate attention of corporate security and legal departments. If audit support is needed, those representing that function should also be advised.

## Accounting and Audit Controls Discourage the Embezzler _____

By way of accounting and audit controls, the embezzler is discouraged from breaching his or her trust through fear of detection and fear of punishment. Detection of embezzlement is possible: (1) through the traditional control concepts of separation of duties and audit trails; (2) through periodic financial and operational audits; (3) through the gathering of intelligence on the lifestyles and personal habits of employees; (4) through allegations and complaints of fellow employees; (5) through the logging of exceptions to prescribed controls and procedures; (6) through the review of variances in operating performance expectations—standards, goals, objectives, budgets, plans, and (7) through the intuition of the embezzler's superiors.

Are there any audit and investigative caveats to embezzlements? Yes, there are several others. First, embezzlers usually do not make "one grand hit" for a million and then run away. They are not "hit and run" criminals like confidence men and women are. Their peculations very often go on for years. And very often their peculations get larger and larger over time. The size of their defalcations usually trips them up. Even a neophyte auditor can detect embezzlement in its later stages.

The second point is that each embezzler has a pattern of theft that is somewhat unique but discernible to an experienced fraud auditor, (for instance, an account category that gets an inordinate amount of "padding" to cover up the loss, a particular step in the audit trail procedures that often gets bypassed, circumvented, or overridden, a favorite customer supplier or contractor whose account balance gets manipulated, or an input document that often is fabricated, counterfeited, or forged). Most long-term embezzlement schemes, after discovery, are found to be very simple. The truly complicated schemes, on the other hand, surface very quickly.

Fraudulent pattern recognition is the unique skill of a trained and experienced fraud auditor. Current efforts to design audit software to duplicate that unique skill, by way of artificial intelligence, are the best hope we now have to stem the tide of computer-related embezzlements.

## The Fringe Benefit Theory of Employee Theft, Fraud, and Embezzlement _____

The difference between legitimate fringe benefits granted to employees by humane employers and workplace larceny by employees at middle and lower levels may be a matter of perception, according to some researchers in criminology. Workers may "look upon some forms of pilferage as harmless, if not actually legitimized by their status as employees." (See Harold R. Holzman and Julia M. Mueller, "Maximizing the Effectiveness of Deterrence as a Control Strategy for Internal Theft," *Journal of Security Administration,* June 1983.)

Employers and employees tend to perceive workplace benefits quite differently. What the employer views as larceny may be looked upon by employees as a perk, unless the employer makes clear what is and what is not a perk, and clearly distinguishes those perks that senior management are entitled to by virtue of their office.

For example, taking hand tools, office supplies, and obsolete inventory items is not considered larceny (theft) by many employees—as long as it isn't done on a daily basis or the total amount of these "takings" is small on an annual basis. Such thefts are construed to be fringe benefits by such employees. They suffer no guilt. If apprehended, they may feel shame, but still no guilt, because they do not believe they have committed a crime, a sin, or an act of disloyalty against their employer.

If you want to further reduce such lower-level theft, you must resort to a different strategy. Apprehension or the fear of apprehension alone will not do it. Enhanced awareness through employee training could. Therefore:

1. Be clear and specific about the company's rules on employee theft, fraud, embezzlement, sabotage, corruption, and information piracy from day one of employment and repeat the message at least annually.

2. Minimize the opportunities to commit such acts by establishing adequate and reasonable internal controls and asset protection measures.

3. When such acts are discovered and the evidence is clear and convincing, let the news of the apprehension become generally known (and don't suggest that the fraud was discovered by accident, but rather on purpose—by audit or security design);

4. Make no apologies for demanding high levels of performance and ethics from employees at all levels.

In addition to an awareness of motives and internal controls, employers must do preemployment checks; learn to recognize activities and behavior of employees that could indicate possible theft; distribute an antitheft policy to employees; bond employees in fiduciary positions; get crime insurance; and talk to an auditor about conducting surprise audits of company financial operations.

## Reminder Checklists

Symptomatic of all frauds:

- An act or actors
- Motivation for commission
- Means for commission
- Opportunity to commit the act
- Opportunity to profit from the act
- The feeling "I won't get caught"

## Crime Motivations List

1. They feel they can get away with it and not be caught.
2. They think they desperately need or want the money or articles stolen.
3. They feel frustrated or dissatisfied about some aspect of their job.

4. They feel frustrated or dissatisfied about some aspect of their personal life that is not job-related.
5. They feel abused by their employers and want to get even.
6. They fail to consider the consequences of being caught.
7. They think, "Everybody else is stealing, so why not me?"
8. They think, "Stealing a little from a big company won't hurt it."
9. They don't know how to manage their own money, so they are always broke and ready to steal.
10. They feel that "beating" the company is a challenge and not a matter of economic gain alone.
11. They were economically, socially, or culturally deprived during childhood.
12. They are compensating for a personal void they feel in their own lives, such as a lack of love, affection, or friendship.
13. They have no self-control. They steal out of compulsion.
14. They feel a friend at work has been subjected to humiliation or abuse or has been treated unfairly.
15. They are just plain lazy and won't work hard to earn enough to buy what they want, need, or desire.
16. The company's internal controls are so lax that everyone is tempted to steal.
17. No one has ever been prosecuted for stealing company property.
18. Most employee thieves are caught by accident rather than by audit or design. Therefore, fear of being caught is not a deterrent to theft.
19. Employees aren't encouraged to discuss personal or financial problems at work or to seek management's advice and counsel on such matters. Besides, it might be embarrassing, an invasion or employee privacy, or could even jeopardize one's career to talk about such things at work.
20. Each theft has its own preceding conditions and each thief has his own motives, so there is no general rule as to why employees steal. It is a situational phenomenon. Therefore, there are many factors which lead an employee to steal, not just a single factor.
21. They steal for any reason the mind and imagination can conjure up.
22. Employees never go to jail or get a harsh sentence for stealing, defrauding, or embezzling from their employers.
23. Man is weak and prone to sin, particularly the sins of pride, lust, envy, anger, covetousness, gluttony, and sloth, all of which may lead to or become motives for theft.
24. Employees today are morally, ethically, and spiritually bankrupt.
25. Employees tend to imitate their bosses. If their bosses steal or cheat, then they are likely to do so also.

## 29 Ways to Steal on the Job

There may be "50 Ways To Leave Your Lover," as Paul Simon sings, but there must be 300 ways to steal from your employer. A few to be aware of follow:

1. Alone
2. With inside co-conspirators
3. With outside co-conspirators
4. By compromising peers
5. By compromising bosses
6. By compromising subordinates
7. By compromising suppliers
8. By compromising contractors
9. By compromising the control system
10. By deceiving the control system
11. By deceiving the bosses
12. By deceiving peers
13. By deceiving subordinates
14. By falsifying documents
15. By falsifying transactions
16. By falsifying entries
17. By falsifying amounts
18. By deleting documents
19. By deleting transactions
20. By deleting entries
21. By bypassing the accounting system
22. By bypassing controls
23. By destroying documents
24. By destroying records
25. By destroying data
26. By destroying files
27. By suppressing exceptions reports
28. By altering, adding, or deleting data
29. By forging or counterfeiting data

## Common Embezzler Profile

- Is a long-time trusted employee.

- Seems to be devoted to the company and job.
- Is very good at his job, but may often operate in a crisis mode—real or faked.
- Lives beyond salary or other obvious means.
- Has compulsive behavior, such as a drug, alcohol, or gambling problem.
- Reluctant to share work tasks related to bookkeeping or the computer.
- Reluctant to take time off or a vacation.
- Has only one or two work references.
- Often has gaps in employment record.
- Usually carries out an embezzlement alone.
- Has embezzled before.

# Law of Embezzlement and Related Crimes

## The Legal Definition of Embezzlement

Embezzlement is the fraudulent appropriation of property by a person to whom it has been entrusted, or to whose possession it has lawfully come. It implies a breach of trust or fiduciary responsibility.

Larceny, a closely related offense, is usually defined as the "wrongful taking and carrying away of the personal property of another with intent to convert it or to deprive the owner of its use and possession." If the taking is by stealth, the crime surreptitiously committed is larceny. If the taking is by guile and deception, by false representation, or by concealment of that which should have been disclosed, the crime charged may be fraud. The major distinction between larceny and embezzlement lies in the issue of the legality of custody of the article stolen. In larceny, the thief never had legal custody. He "feloniously took" the article stolen. In embezzlement, the thief is legally authorized by the owner to take or receive the article and to possess it for a time. The formulation of intent to steal the article may occur subsequent to the time when it came into his possession or concurrently with initial possession. If initial possession and intent to steal occur simultaneously, the crime is larceny. If intent to steal occurs subsequent to initial possession, the crime is embezzlement. The essence of embezzlement, then, lies in the breach of a fiduciary relationship deriving from the entrustment of money.

## Federal Statutes on Embezzlement

There are 70 federal criminal statutes covering elements of embezzlement, from labor unions and federal funds to local agencies and commodity exchanges, plus a broad range of federal property.

Most prosecutions occur under the following criminal statutes:

- 18 U.S.C. 641 covers larceny, embezzlement, or conversion of public monies or property of the United States.
- 18 U.S.C. 656 covers theft, embezzlement or misapplication of a bank's money, funds, or credit willfully by an [officer, employee, or others connected to] with intent to injure or defraud a national bank, federally insured bank or branch or agency of a foreign bank. Section 657 covers lending, credit, and insurance institutions.
- 18 U.S.C. 1344 covers financial institution fraud; scheme or artifice to defraud a federally insured institution to take money, funds, credits, assets, securities, or other property by misrepresentation.
- 18 U.S.C. 1344 reads as follows:

  (a) Whoever knowingly executes, or attempts to execute, a scheme or artifice—(1) to defraud a financial institution; or (2) to obtain any of the moneys, funds, credits, assets, securities or other property owned by or under the custody or control of a financial institution by means of false or fraudulent pretenses, representations, or promises, shall be fined not more than $1,000,000, or imprisoned not more than 30 years, or both.

Under the Crime Control Act of 1990, Congress lengthened the statute of limitations for bank fraud to ten years.

A recent statute, 18 U.S.C. 1033, makes it a federal offense to commit insurance fraud or to embezzle from the finances of an insurance company engaged in interstate commerce. An expansion of the concept of embezzlement is willful misapplication that requires only the temporary taking or use of funds by the defendant or a third party.

## Labor Laws

The Labor Management Reporting and Disclosure Act of 1959 (29 U.S.C. 501) prohibits the embezzlement of union funds by labor officials. Title V, "Safeguards for Labor Organizations" imposes a fiduciary duty on all union officers, prohibits embezzlement, and requires bonding coverage against loss by acts of fraud or dishonesty committed by officers.

## Federal Sentencing Guidelines for Embezzlement

The applicable guideline section for federal embezzlement offenses is found in Part B of the Federal Sentencing Guidelines, "Offenses Involving Property; Larceny, Embezzlement and Other Forms of Theft," 2B1.1.

The highest level offense is a level 24, which is an offense that "substantially jeopardized the safety and soundness of a financial institution; or affected a financial institution and the defendant derived more than $1,000,000 in gross receipts from the offense."

The offense would have to make the financial institution insolvent; or, cause a situation in which the institution "substantially reduced benefits to pensioners or insured persons; was unable on demand to refund fully any deposit, payment or investment; was so depleted of its assets as to be forced to merge with another institution in order to continue active operations; or was placed in substantial jeopardy of any of the above."

## Other Statutes Relevant to Embezzlement and Prosecution _____

### Forgery

An embezzlement often involves forged documents, and the law of forgery (the material altering of a document with the intent to defraud) comes into play. Forgery may also be the entry of false passwords into a computer to gain access and use the computer to defraud.

### Conspiracy

The act of conspiracy consists of the following: two or more persons must agree to commit a criminal act; the agreement need only be inferred; at least one party to the conspiracy must perform some act in furtherance of the conspiracy (this act need not be criminal); one party may be held responsible for the acts of his co-conspirators even though he did not commit any substantive offenses or have actual knowledge of them—a partnership in crime includes all members within its scope and during its time of operation. The agreement must be to either violate a criminal statute or, under federal law, to defraud the U.S. government. The definition of fraud is not limited to that of common law; the federal statute includes every conspiracy to impair, obstruct, or defeat any lawful function of the government.

## Criminal Statutes Often Merged with Conspiracy _____

### Mail Fraud

Under the mail fraud statute (18 U.S.C. 1341) the government needs to prove a "scheme or artifice to defraud, or for obtaining money or property by means of false or fraudulent pretenses, representations, or promises," and to use the mails for delivery/execution of the scheme.

The scheme can be executed by one or more persons; with two or more involved there is a conspiracy to defraud. Each defendant is subject to mail fraud counts and "shall be fined not more than $1,000 or imprisoned not more than five years, or both."

### Wire Fraud

The essential elements of wire fraud (18 U.S.C. 1343) are: (1) the devising of a scheme and artifice to defraud; and (2) a transmittal in interstate or foreign commerce by means of wire, radio, or television communication of writings, signs, signals, pictures or sounds for the purpose of executing the scheme and artifice to defraud. Here is where transmission of computer data over telephone lines fits.

The statute provides:

> *Whoever, having devised or intending to devise any scheme or artifice to defraud, or for obtaining money or property by means of false or fraudulent pretenses, representations or promises, transmits or causes to be transmitted*

*by means of wire, radio, or television communication in interstate or foreign commerce, any writings, signs, signals, pictures, or sounds for the purpose of executing such scheme or artifice, shall be fined not more than $1,000 or imprisoned not more than five years, or both.*

## Money Laundering

The Money Laundering Control Act of 1986 (18 USC 1956 to 1957) was passed in October 1986 as part of the Anti-Drug Abuse Act of 1986. The Act created two new offenses related to money laundering and currency transaction reporting violations.

Reporting requirements are required for parties engaged in certain cash transactions; specifically:

- Banks and financial institutions must report transactions of $10,000 or more in cash in a single transaction or related transactions.
- Persons transporting monetary instruments into or out of the U.S.
- Financial institutions must verify the identity of persons who purchase bank checks, traveler' s checks, or money orders in amounts of $3,000 or more.
- A Foreign Bank Account Report is required whenever a person has an account in a foreign bank of more than $5,000 in value.

Treasury regulations require a paper trail of bank records that must be maintained for up to five years.

# Chapter 4

# An Embezzler's Guide to Your Computer

Computers offer embezzlers with some computing and accounting skills an easy way to steal and to make their crime harder to detect and prosecute.

Employers enhance the opportunity for embezzlement by having most or all financial operations on the computer, putting one person in charge, and having lax internal financial controls or none at all.

## The Embezzlement Environment

Computer-related embezzlement schemes differ from other embezzlement methods in at least one important regard. The use of computer systems makes it possible for thieves to steal more money more quickly—and to leave comparatively little evidence of their acts.

Embezzlement, like all crimes, is a product of motive and opportunity. Opportunity is created through the absence of or weaknesses in internal controls. Embezzlers are adept at finding a company's control weaknesses. All an embezzler needs is control of the computer, or of one or more of its financial operations, such as payroll or accounts payable.

In some instances, opportunity is motive: some embezzlers seize easy opportunities for theft through a computer because they are easy to seize, whereas other types of embezzlers steal because of the challenge of limited opportunities imposed by strong controls. However, the motivation for most perpetrators of computer-related embezzlement is the same as for other types of embezzlement.

## Fraud In, Fraud Out

Computers, in their management-assistance role, can provide instantaneous information necessary to monitor inventories, process orders, issue purchase orders, and bill customers. While the computer can do all this and more, there is still the need for checks and controls of the computerized systems as well as of the manual processes. These checks and controls are needed simply because it is humans who enter the initial data into the computer. And humans can and do make mistakes and are prone to steal.

There can be no fully computerized system simply because someone—not a machine—must control, instruct, and feed data into the computer. The computer is, essentially, a logical but indiscriminate machine; that is, it doesn't question the data it receives (although it may reject it), and it will simply follow instructions and turn out what it is told to turn out. It is the nature of the computer, how and why it operates with its human interface, that forces manual checks and controls.

If the wrong data are put into the computer it operates on the "GIGO" principle, "Garbage In, Garbage Out." We need another acronym for criminal manipulation of the computer: FIFO, or Fraud In, Fraud Out.

As an example, let's examine the interrelations between manual and computerized controls in an inventory system and how these controls can be audited. Although the use of computers is widespread, there are usually areas in any operation in which manual intervention is necessary to complete the required process. For example, in the receiving department, a clerk may have to verify by sight the quantity of the merchandise received and log this information on a receiving report document. Most audits of these functions are straightforward—is the clerk performing the necessary checks and logging the correct information? But what about the link from the receiving report to computerized records? What about the computer program that is supposed to make sure that the amount received equals the amount ordered?

Just as a receiving clerk can easily give "special" attention to preferred vendors, so can the computer programmer. Instructions can be generated so that edits are bypassed for "special" vendors; or for certain items, the balance-on-hand might be shorted in anticipation of later thefts. Whatever the technique, the result is the same: serious losses for the company. That is why audits of computerized operations must be done regularly.

Does the computer program actually perform its function? Does controlled input generate predictable output? Do output listings really reflect the processing that took place? Are all computer file updates logged for future audit requirements? And of course, for this example, the final check is the verification that the manual system matches the computerized records. That is, does the physical inventory match the computerized inventory?

## Fraud Is Where You Find It

A fraudulent entry, to be detectable in a computerized accounting system, must be sensed (seen, heard, felt, tasted, or smelled) by man or machine; that is, an auditor or the system itself. The system cannot audit itself until the auditor shares with it his or her knowledge, skills, wisdom, and experience. What is it that a fraud auditor knows, does, senses, and perceives? And just as important as the auditor's base of knowledge, skill, and experience, what does a typical defrauder know, do, sense, or perceive? Why should we care about the defrauder? Because fraud surfaces more often by coincidence (accident) than by audit purpose or design. If we can better understand the defrauder's psyche, we may be able to detect his or her frauds sooner.

Defrauders—successful ones, at least—who fear discovery attempt to make their fraudulent entries look or appear normal by any control criteria (for instance, the amount is within established limits, the entry originator is authorized, the account classifications are proper, the place and timing of the transaction are appropriate as are the transacting parties, and the subject matter of the transaction is fitting to the needs of the business). That is asking a lot from a typical defrauder; many of them bypass the accounting system completely if they can. They take their money or other things of value without subverting the accounting system to cover it up. Others sell assets for full value, alter the document of sale to a lesser value for a fabricated reason, and then pocket the difference. Others find clever ways to manipulate weaknesses in the accounting and control systems so that their peculations appear to be within the bounds of the weak standards, policies, procedures, and exceptions criteria.

To cover up their activities, for example, embezzlers typically create misinformation or disinformation, destroy information, suppress information or utilize rationalizations if authenticity or accuracy of an entry is challenged. They dream up stories that can justify their entries and thereby create a form of plausible deniability. ("Who, me steal? Why should I? My uncle left me all this money. That's how I can afford my Rolls Royce on a salary of $30,000.")

If we were to program a computer to audit itself for the possibility of fraud, we would first provide a mechanism for the system to screen out people who are not authorized to have any form of access. Then we would layer the legitimate users according to their job responsibilities and information needs; that is, assign access rights by security level. Next, to protect the system from legitimate users who might exceed their authority, we would provide a mechanism for the system to audit its users for security violations (in other words, accessing information for which they have no right or need to know). We now have technologies that can accomplish these control objectives relatively well.

When we move into the realm of fraud prevention controls, we are left with monitoring individual system users according to their profile of legitimate uses, such as their defined program and file access rights and privileges and their prespecified and expected transaction characteristics. These are then monitored either continuously or on a sampling basis for deviation from security standards, acceptable accounting practice, and other control criteria like transaction amount, timing, frequency, volume, mathematical accuracy, modification of programs, files, logs, and so on.

Doing all that, do we now have an adequate fraud prevention mechanism? We have about as much prevention as technology can provide today. But detecting fraudulent entries, either by eyeball or by computer, is a micro approach. It addresses fraud from the perspective of a user who is highly constrained by controls imposed on the system by higher authorities, who in and of themselves may not be so constrained. The defrauder then must overcome that obstacle by such techniques as impersonation, masking, masquerading, or disguising himself or the transaction.

The assumption is that fraud is an act accomplished by an individual—one person. What about fraudulent conspiracies? How can they be detected?

Conspiracy may be tougher to discover, particularly if at least one conspirator has a high level of authority and can bypass or waive controls. Here the system may always appear to be in balance. There are no traditional red flags as there are for errant individual users. We must look more broadly at the problem of fraud; that is, look to its environmental rather than its individual characteristics—give it a macro look.

## Reminder Checklists

### Elements That Help the Embezzler in Computer Embezzlement

1. Some knowledge of bookkeeping and accounting.
2. Some knowledge of the computer system.
3. Opportunity to control of all or most functions or programs of the computer system.
4. Lax or absent effective internal and financial controls.
5. Management attitude that is anti-controls and safeguards or that views controls as a hindrance to operations.
6. Belief that a computer crime is hard to detect, investigate, and prosecute.
7. Opportunity to profit from the embezzlement.

### Four Distinctive Features of Computer-related Embezzlement Schemes

1. They are committed generally by people with suitable skills in computer operations or in information systems auditing. (However, it has proved possible for someone who is completely unskilled in computing to steal significant amounts from an information processing application.)
2. These embezzlement schemes are carried out most often by exploiting deficiencies in an application's existing internal controls. (These weaknesses may stem from defects in the design or installation of the controls themselves, negligence in enforcing them consistently, or a failure to monitor and follow up expeditiously on their operation.)
3. Computer-related embezzlements can be executed at any of the three stages of the transaction processing flow—that is, during input, throughput, or output. The most common thefts that have been uncovered are those

executed in the input stage, during which false, forged, or altered data are entered.

4. These embezzlement schemes most commonly are directed against accounts payable, payroll, and benefit or expense claims.

## Red Flags: Common Computer Embezzlement Scams

The embezzler uses the computer to carry out the crime, to manipulate the accounting system and its controls. The most common method is a form of input scam involving the submission of false and fraudulent vendor invoices, expense claims, salary claims, and benefit claims for payment.

The easiest way to "beat" an accounting system is through the creation of a fake debit by way of a phony claim from an alleged vendor, alleged employee, or alleged benefit claimant. The claimant is usually spurious or nonexistent, or real but not entitled to payment. Phony expense claims are for real claimants but are either completely fabricated or overinflated.

To make an accounts payable scam work, for example, an embezzler would need to be able to:

1. Get a phony vendor on the approved vendor list. (Someone in purchasing, or with authority to approve new vendors, would have to be compromised, or access to a new vendor authorization form would have to be secured and the authorization forged, or access to the approved vendor master file would have to be accessed and amended by adding the phony vendor.)

2. Get access to purchase order requisition forms to fabricate a requisition (forge the signature of someone with authority to issue such forms).

3. Issue a fraudulent purchase order (PO). A surreptitious theft of pre-serially numbered purchase orders would be required and authorization to issue the PO would have to be faked or forged. (If POs are not prenumbered, it is easier to accomplish this kind of fraud. Random numbers could be used for the purchase orders. In a computerized system however, with proper programming controls, a purchase order whose number is random or out of current sequencing would be "flagged" as an exception. This is called a sequence check.)

4. Fabricate a receiving report showing delivery of the goods.

5. Fabricate a vendor invoice for the amount of the goods allegedly received.

6. Fabricate an account number or expense category to be charged for the alleged purchase.

7. Issue a fabricated check requisition or check voucher.

Looking at all the steps involved in perpetrating a fraud of this type might cause one to assume that successful frauds are rarities. They are not. Disbursement-type frauds are rather commonplace and certainly the most frequent of all employee frauds.

The reason why such frauds occur with regularity is that despite what look like airtight control procedures, each control and procedure can be compromised or bypassed. The assumption inherent in all accounting and internal controls is that some order exists in the organization and that time is always available to process items in accordance with good, sound control principles. But controls hinder processing. The payment of bills can be greatly expedited if no controls are present, so trade-offs are continually being made when backlogs develop or emergencies arise. In such circumstances, controls get compromised by the exigencies of the moment. So in designing accounting and control systems, deviations from normal processing steps, which permit compromises or overrides of the control procedures, are allowed for. These exceptions to the general rule are what serve as the inspiration for fraud.

For example, when a critical part is necessary for the completion of a manufactured article, the purchasing department may be instructed to buy it anywhere, from anyone, whether approved as a vendor or not. Adding the vendor's name to the approved vendor master file may follow actual receipt of the parts, rather than preceding that step.

A large order from a new customer may be so vital to the company's cash flow that normal credit checking procedures are bypassed. Or a large customer may demand immediate shipment of goods, even before an invoice is properly prepared. And inventory control records may be so far behind in postings that requisitions are issued for goods that are in large supply already.

Again, these deviations or exceptions are what the criminal attempts to exploit. Chaos is his or her stock in trade. Instead of fabricating six or seven documents, the criminal creates an emergency event to justify the overriding or bypassing of controls.

Expenditure controls for routine purchases may be quite effective, because the charge is to the current year's budget. But capital expenditures come from another budgetary control, the long-range plan or budget. Here the signature of one person, that of the controller or financial vice president, may be the only requirement for check issuance. A fabricated invoice presented to that one person may be all it takes to get an "offline" check issued to a spurious provider of corporate services, if the "story" accompanying the request is some sort of feigned emergency, for example, the vendor needs an advance to buy materials, or expedite construction, or to acquire vital equipment. The only other control might be that the amount of the check is within the check requester's capital budget and that its alleged purpose lies in an area of the business for which the check requester has responsibility, such as maintenance, construction, or office equipment.

# Inventory Scams: Conversions, Embezzlement, and Collusion

While the cash and receivables scams mainly involve clerical or white-collar workers, inventory conversions mainly involve collusion of blue-collar factory and warehouse employees, truck drivers, and sometimes even company vendors who corrupt these people. The perpetrators, number, variety, and complexity of inventory frauds are impossible to estimate, assess, or catalog. The design of such scams is a neverending process. The following are but a few:

- Arbitrarily reclassifying inventory to a no-value or limited-value category. (Examples include damaged, obsolete, sample, "freebie", back-ordered, re-shipment of lost or misdelivered goods, a substitute for out-of-stock goods previously paid for by a customer, and so forth.)
- Undercounted goods on the receiving side; overcounted goods on the shipping side of the warehouse.
- Throwing perfectly good material into a dumpster and later reclaiming it when no one is around.
- Accepting short weights or counts from a salvage operator who has contracted to buy scrap from the plant at higher than competitive prices—then splitting the ill-gotten proceeds.

## Legal Definitions

A conversion, legally, is an unauthorized act that deprives an owner of his property permanently or for an indefinite time. Federal law (18 U.S.C. 641) covers larceny, embezzlement, or conversion of public monies or property of the United States. And the Economic Espionage Act of 1996, designed to protect proprietary economic information, has criminal penalties for the theft, unauthorized appropriation or conversion, duplication, alteration, destruction, wrongful copying, or control of trade secrets, or the wrongful diversion of a trade secret to the economic benefit of someone other than its owners, or some disadvantage to the rightful owners.

## Inventory System Controls

Although the use of computers and bar code systems is widespread, there are usually areas in any inventory operation where manual intervention is necessary to complete the required process. For example, outdated bar code scanners may break down and be unable to read. Data may have to be entered on keypads, which means there's bound to be a certain number of errors. Or in the receiving department, a clerk may have to sight verify the quantity of the merchandise received and log this information on a receiving report document. Most audits of these functions are straightforward—is the clerk performing the necessary checks and logging the correct information? But what about the link from receiving report to computerized records? What about the computer program that is supposed to make sure that the amount received equals the amount ordered?

What if the system is batch-based and data have to be uploaded daily to a computer? What if there's a system crash and that day's data are lost?

Known weaknesses in the computer system are what thieves look to exploit; or, perhaps they may seek to cause an "accident" such as a system crash to create an opportunity for theft.

Just as a receiving clerk can easily give "special" attention to preferred vendors, so can the computer operator. Instructions can be generated so that edits are bypassed for "special" vendors; or for certain items, the balance-on-hand might be shorted in anticipation of later thefts. Whatever the technique, the result is the same: serious losses for the company.

Does the computer program actually perform its function? Does controlled input generate predictable output? Do output listings really reflect the processing that took place? Are all computer file updates logged for future audit requirements? And of course, for this example, the final check is the verification that the manual system matches the computerized records. That is, does the physical inventory match the computerized inventory?

Companies of substantial size normally have purchasing departments whose role is to secure the best goods, materials, supplies, merchandise, and services at the best prices available. In order to fulfill that role properly a number of controls are built into the purchasing process:

First of all, lists of approved vendors must be kept and maintained. Second, procedures should be designed to ensure that:

- On very large purchases, bids are solicited from at least three approved vendors.
- Purchase orders are issued only on the basis of a signed requisition from an authorized department head.
- Purchase order blank forms are pre-serially numbered, kept under the control of one person and, for manual systems, stored away safely.

- Buyers (purchasing agents) be periodically rotated so that relationships between them and their vendors do not get too cozy, because objectivity can be compromised as can integrity over a period of time.
- Purchase orders be signed by a purchasing agent or other responsible purchasing official.
- Copies of the purchase order are distributed to the vendor, along with the receiving, accounts payable, and the order originating departments.
- Purchasing department personnel be prohibited from acknowledging receipt of goods or authorizing payment for goods received (the separation of duties principle).

When the goods are received, the receiving department matches the purchase order with the goods delivered to verify counts, weight and other product specifications, as well as the physical condition of the contents. (Quality control may also selectively inspect the goods to verify grade, quality, and standard specifications as to composition, as well as to update the vendor's quality control file regarding timely delivery, correct counts and weights, and correct grade or quality.)

The receiving department then acknowledges receipt and distributes copies of its report to the purchasing department to relieve the open purchase order file, to accounts payable for invoice and check processing, to the stores department for further handling and storage, and/or to the inventory control department to update its stock records.

In smaller companies these tasks, however, are not always separated. Occasionally, one or more employees may have dual responsibilities, for instance, physical access to both assets and accounting records. This may create a serious internal control problem. Add to that the movement toward small companies utilizing minicomputers and the consequent loss of paper trail documents, and you have a situation ripe for employee skullduggery of all sorts.

# *Accounting Procedural Security Questionnaire*

## Inventory Shrinkage _____

1. Determine the variation between perpetual inventory records and the actual inventory for the preceding three annual accounting periods:

| *Year* | *Inventory/Books* | *Inventory/Count* | *$ Variation* | *% Variation* |
|--------|-------------------|-------------------|---------------|---------------|
| ____ | _____ | _____ | _____ | _____ |
| ____ | _____ | _____ | _____ | _____ |
| ____ | _____ | _____ | _____ | _____ |

2. Is there a predetermined annual date for the physical inventory count?

3. Is the annual date for the count staggered from year to year?

4. How much advance notice is given of the date for the physical count to:

- Accounting personnel?

- Top company executives?

- Company supervisors?

- Computer personnel?

5. What percentage of the total dollar value of the inventory per books is involved in the physical count?

6. How long are inventory tags kept after completion of the count, particularly unused tags?

7. Are tags pre-serially numbered?

8. Are all tags accounted for after the inventory is taken?

- Are all differences reconciled?

- How?

- By whom?

9. Who has personal custody of unused tags?

- Does that person also order the tags?

- Identify the tag supplier:

10. Who has personal custody of used tags?

11. What controls are used to cut off further issuance and preparation of tags after the count is completed?

## Accounts Payable Procedures_____

1. Describe in detail the internal control procedures to verify incoming shipments (if a bar code/symbol receiving system is used, describe the system):

2. Identify the persons authorized to make gross counts on incoming shipments or perform other types of freight bill verification:

3. Identify the persons authorized to make net counts on incoming shipments, including the packing slip, invoice, or purchase order verification:

4. Identify the persons who weigh, count, and/or inspect the quality of contents of individual containers:

5. Describe in detail the manual and/or computerized flow of all verification and receiving documents after a shipment has been received, checked, and stored, including freight bills, packing slips, invoices (if any), receiving reports, purchase orders, storage orders, transfers, etc.:

6. Does any supervisory personnel test-check gross counts, net counts, and authorization of personnel who verify receipt of goods? If so, identify supervisors:

7. How often are errors detected by supervisors in gross count?

   • Net count?

   • Quality specifications?

   • Authority of person making count:

8. Are freight bills attached to or matched with specific receiving reports?

9. Is a matching procedure used to compare freight bills and receiving reports?

   • Receiving reports and packing slips?

- Packing slips and purchase orders?

- Purchase orders and invoices?

- Invoices and check vouchers?

10. At what point in the document processing (outlined in 9 above) is the journal entry made which adds the part(s) or items to the current perpetual inventory balance?

11. Describe recordkeeping procedures after goods are verified and transferred from receiving department to warehousing department:

12. Describe the receiving procedures for handling deliveries, when quantity is less than purchase order specifies:

- When delivery is less than packing slips specify:

- When goods delivered do not meet quality specifications, carton count specifications, or the specifications of the goods called for in the purchase order:

13. Does accounts payable section authorize payment on an invoice when less than total delivery has been made? If so, under what conditions?

14. Who authorizes check disbursements for invoices? What documentation is required before checks are issued?

15. Do intra-company shipments vary from any of the above procedures? If so, describe differences:

16. Prepare and attach a schematic diagram of the flow of all documentation involved in purchasing, receiving, and warehousing operations:

17. Are the above documents kept after payment of the invoice? If so, for how long a period?

# Accounts Receivable Procedures _____

1. Describe in detail the internal control procedures for handling outbound shipments:

2. What documentation is required to authorize withdrawals from stock?

3. What documentation is required before inventory is removed from stock and prepared for shipment?

4. Who is authorized to issue shipping orders? Stock withdrawals?

5. Who is authorized to determine whether materials or inventory are in such condition that they should be scrapped? Salvaged? Repaired? Deemed obsolete?

6. Who selects scrap or salvage firms?

7. Does competitive bidding exist for scrap or salvage removal?

8. What is the approximate annual cost of scrapped goods?

9. What is the approximate annual revenue derived from scrap sales?

10. Describe in detail how sales orders are handled before loading:

11. What documentation is required before warehouse personnel pick goods to fill sales orders?

12. Are sales orders rechecked before loading? By whom?

13. Is the truck car locked immediately after loading is completed?

14. Prepare and attach a schematic diagram of the flow of all documentation involved in the sale and shipment of goods:

15. Are "no charge" sales ever made? Who authorizes them?

16. Are no charge withdrawals ever made from inventory? If so, under what conditions?

17. Are back order logs kept?

18. Are back orders a chronic problem? Why?

19. If less than a full shipment is made, is the customer invoiced for the full order or for that portion of the order actually shipped?

20. Are intra-company sales handled differently than sales to customers? If so, how?

21. Who authorizes accounts receivable write-offs? Under what conditions or circumstances?

# Five Key Management Defenses to Embezzlement

## 1. Fostering Management Awareness and Attitude

The five key defenses against embezzlement all flow from the owners and managers of the organization and their fiduciary duty to protect the entity's assets. Management must believe not only that fraud, theft, and embezzlement exist and that their organization could become a victim, but also that controls and safeguards can reduce the opportunity for embezzlement, and that these need to be monitored and enforced.

## 2. Practicing Preventive Law

The protection and preservation of a firm's assets (human, capital, technological, and information) from the foreseeable consequences of acts of God (namely, climatic catastrophes), acts of the public enemy (property theft, fraud, embezzlement, sabotage, information piracy, commercial corruption) and human errors and omissions (employee negligence, design flaw, mechanical failure), are made the peculiar responsibility of a corporation's officers, directors, and agents by a host of federal, state, and local laws, such as the Foreign Corrupt Practices Act, Occupational Safety and Health Act, Equal Employment Opportunity Act, the Privacy Act, the Employee Retirement Income Security Act of 1974 (ERISA), incorporation statutes, worker's compensation laws, building and fire safety codes, product liability laws, and the general common law of contracts, agency, torts, and fiduciary responsibility.

Officers and directors of public companies are now keenly aware of these responsibilities. The point is often brought home to them by actions initiated by the Securities and Exchange Commission, as well as by lawsuits initiated by irate stockholders and creditors, employees, environmentalists, state and local authorities, and community organizations. Officers and directors must therefore exercise discretion, good business judgment, and due diligence in their management of company assets and business operations. Any failure in exercising care may subject them to lawsuits by damaged parties. The exercise of prudent business judgment would therefore dictate that enlightened members of top management undertake from time to time, a serious review of the adequacy of asset protection plans, policies, procedures, and controls.

Such a review is important for several reasons, first, as a defensive measure, to assure top management that reasonable and adequate precautions have in fact been taken; second, as a prevention measure to detect new areas of control weaknesses and vulnerabilities that may require administrative action or correction; and third, as an offensive measure to reduce losses and insurance premiums.

## The Breadth of Fiduciary Liability

Besides a grasp of the law relating to fraud and embezzlement, management should be cognizant of the liability that can attach to the organization and its personnel from not taking steps to deter and detect embezzlement and theft. The important concepts are negligence and duty of care as they relate to assets protection. Failure to protect assets could leave officers or owners open to charges of contributory negligence should a critical loss occur.

The responsible corporate officer doctrine applies to any corporate officer or employee "standing in responsible relation" to a forbidden act. Liability can arise if the officer could have prevented or corrected a violation and failed to do so. Strict liability focuses on act only, no mental element is involved.

This is a critical doctrine with significant implications. An officer has a positive duty to seek out and remedy violations when they occur and a duty to implement measures that will ensure that violations will not occur. The doctrine forces the corporate officer to define which risks he should know, because he is likely to be held to an affirmative duty of care concerning those risks.

The broad test of negligence, as defined in *American Jurisprudence* 2d, Section 135, is what a "reasonably prudent person would foresee and would do in the light of this foresight under the circumstances."

Let's take a specific example of another level of negligence as it relates to embezzlement and forgery. If an employee embezzles by forging company checks, the company may be able to get reimbursed by the bank that accepted the forged check. The bank, however, could refuse and claim the company was negligent in several areas, such as giving the employee access to the checkbooks, signing partially completed checks, or not securing the automatic check signer. The Uniform Commercial Code, Section 3-406, spells out types of negligence associated with financial documents and bank customer liability for check fraud.

One can see how a crippling loss or bankruptcy of the company could lead to legal action against the company and its officers, by employees or shareholders charging negligent hiring and retention, failure to supervise, and failure to establish and monitor effective financial controls.

## 3. Developing Policies and Codes of Conduct _____

In attempting to reduce theft, an important task of management is to express clearly to employees that theft is considered to be and will be treated as a serious problem. A crucial first step toward this end is to include the topic of employee theft as a matter for organizational policy.

The major consequence of a theft policy is the meaning it conveys to employees. A corporate antitheft stance can reinforce general societal and legal norms within the organization. Although one could argue that societal prohibitions against stealing are already quite explicit, it is also true that the actual implementation of such standards in specific situations is much less clear.

By showing concern for theft, corporate officials can demonstrate that the taking of company property is considered to be theft and will be dealt with as a serious problem. A strong policy emphasis may also serve to deter theft behavior. Simply stated, the deterrence perspective is based on a model of "rational man." Persons will avoid a behavior if the costs for engaging in it are greater than the benefits to be derived from it. Applied to theft and embezzlement, this "utility" framework suggests that stealing will be eliminated if employees expect that the punishments for theft will outweigh any possible gains. The role of policy in this regard is to help establish a climate in which incidents of theft will not be tolerated or treated lightly. Obviously, other factors such as security also contribute to this climate and must be examined for a more complete understanding of the dynamics of deterrence in an organization.

## 4. Establishing Controls and Audits_____

Management is responsible for internal controls. Internal accounting controls have been defined in law, legislation, regulation, and standards as referring to those controls that assure the accurate reporting of financial information. Chapter 11, on internal controls, gives a detailed description of these requirements. The function of the auditor is to examine and attest to the accuracy of the financial information of an organization.

There are different kinds of internal controls, control systems, and control techniques. We can define seven elements, in combination, that make up internal control:

1. Organization control
2. System development and change control
3. Authorization and reporting controls
4. Accounting system controls
5. Security and safeguards controls
6. Management supervisory controls
7. Documentation controls

In each of the above areas, control techniques can either be formal or informal. Formal mechanisms are usually those that can be audited without too much difficulty. Informal mechanisms are more difficult to audit since they include concepts or standards such as leadership, organization structure, ethical guidelines, or trade practices.

## 5. Having Adequate Insurance Protection _____

Employee dishonesty insurance and fidelity bonding complement internal controls, audits, and careful employee screening and selection.

The purpose of fidelity bonds is to indemnify the employer for loss of money or other property sustained through dishonest acts of his bonded personnel. The scope of acts insured against includes embezzlement committed by the employee, whether that person is acting alone or in collusion with others.

Bear in mind that the fidelity bond is not an employee dishonesty form. Loss must result from dishonesty on the part of the bonded employee. The employee should be bonded in an amount adequate to offset potential thefts and with not too high a deductible.

Be aware that under the ERISA of 1974, every organization that comes under the act is required to carry employee dishonesty insurance for every trustee, officer, employee, or administrator who handles funds or property of a pension benefit plan.

# Chapter 8

# Insurance Against Embezzlement

The securing of appropriate and comprehensive insurance protection and coverage for the risk of embezzlement is a very important line of defense. Employee dishonesty insurance and fidelity bonds are not a substitute for internal and accounting controls, but internal controls and audits do not necessarily prevent and detect employee dishonesty and losses. Insurance and controls are complementary to a large degree.

## Reasons for Dishonesty Insurance

The purpose of employee dishonesty insurance is to indemnify the employer for loss of money or other property sustained through dishonest acts of his or her bonded personnel. The scope of acts insured against may include: larceny, theft of money and securities, embezzlement, forgery or alteration, misappropriation, wrongful abstraction, willful misapplication, extortion, counterfeit currency, computer systems fraud, or other fraudulent and dishonest acts committed by the employee, whether acting alone or in collusion with others. Bear in mind that the fidelity bond is not an all-risk form. Loss must result from dishonesty on the part of the bonded employee. That which is caused by omission or error not involving dishonesty is not covered.

## Coverage

Property, real or personal—including money—is covered, whether owned by the employer or belonging to others. If the employee had access to funds or if he is authorized to buy, sell, ship or store goods, he should be bonded in an amount adequate to offset potential thefts. It is logical enough that the larger the firm's assets and the greater the turnover in volume of business, the more probable that a larger loss or series of losses may be concealed for a long period.

The insurance is written on a schedule basis, that is, to cover employees by name or position, or on a blanket coverage of all employees.

Under the Employee Retirement Income Security Act of 1974 (ERISA) every company subject to its provisions is required to have employee dishonesty insurance for anyone handling an employer-sponsored welfare or pension benefit plan, including the plan sponsor, administrator, trustee, officer, or employee who handles funds or other property of the plan.

## Required Proof

To satisfy a claim, circumstantial evidence must show that the employee intended to defraud or embezzle (in other words, committed a voluntary act resulting in direct financial gain).

The "manifest intent" clause of policies can be shown when a particular result is certain to follow from an employee's conduct. However, there must be more than mistake, carelessness, or incompetence.

## Notice

The notice provision is included in nearly every insurance policy, and it is a potential pitfall in obtaining coverage for claims. Under an insurance policy, notice is required to the insurance company of a claim for recovery. Failure to satisfy this requirement can result in no indemnification for an otherwise covered claim.

The notice provision is usually in the "conditions" section of a policy. Terms often used to define notice are: "as soon as practicable" after an incident that could be eligible for a claim; "as soon thereafter" as the insured has knowledge of an incident; or "immediately."

Notice is often not given or delayed because the insured is not sure of the proper insurance policy under which to make a claim, or is ignorant of the policy coverage, lacks knowledge of the incident, or does not believe a claim will arise.

However, once it is determined notice should be given for a claim, it is best to inform the insurance company as quickly as possible. In fact, even if the organization is unsure that its insurance will cover a claim, it is still best to notify the insurance company of the possible claim.

## Nine Steps in Recovery for Losses

1. Consult with your attorney or insurance broker to:
- Identify the specific policy under which you can file a claim.
- Clarify the meanings of specific clauses relating to notice, termination, subrogation (settlement) remedies, and proof of loss as well as the time frame for submitting that proof according to your specific policy.
- Identify what types of damages are excluded in your policy.
2. Immediately send notice of loss to your broker/agent.

3. Investigate the possible loss:

- Use internal auditors, security, and legal personnel, or go to an outside investigative agency specializing in internal employee theft and embezzlement. Cooperate with insurance company investigators at the appropriate point.
- Identify and interview all staff with knowledge of the embezzlement.
- Identify documents, electronic media, and other materials that might be relevant to determining loss or identifying guilty parties.
- Determine the extent of the loss and if any assets are retrievable.

4. Terminate the dishonest employee(s)—only on the advice of legal counsel and if your policy has a termination clause that excludes coverage if you retain a dishonest employee.

5. Submit proof of loss to the insurance company.

6. Again, cooperate with your insurance company; do not let it charge that your company failed to cooperate with the investigation or in any other way. However, consult with your attorney about the nature of your cooperation, especially about the confidentiality of documents.

7. Do not settle with any party without discussing it with your insurance company.

8. Present accurate and provable/auditable losses in your fidelity claim.

9. Be prepared to sue your insurance company if your claim is denied.

# Designing Effective Policies

This chapter provides a policy framework and describes how policies can be a focus for defining core company values and goals, which then can be implemented through standards, guidelines, and performance indicators. Through polices, a company can assert its prerogative to supervise and ensure an efficient and secure operation and to protect its interests.

The overall goals are to produce policies that provide clear, accurate, and persuasive communication on required conduct for employees. Policies are a means of educating employees on ethical and legal obligations, which may, in turn, reduce potential litigation risks for the company. These policies also foster a company climate of recognizing an obligation to obey laws and of not tolerating acts that skirt or breach laws. Finally, this focus on policy will allow a review of your current company policy on internal theft or embezzlement, or help you to save the time, money, and frustration associated with developing a policy from scratch.

## Policies from the Top Down

Organizations that have a board of directors may produce executive limitations policies to ensure that the chief executive officer carries out his duties in a prudent and ethical manner.

For example, the board may direct the CEO to prevent corporate assets—intellectual property and proprietary information assets may be specifically cited along with physical and financial assets—from being unprotected or unnecessarily placed at risk, to keep the company's public image from being endangered, or to avoid taking any action that is imprudent or unethical.

## Ethics and Codes of Conduct

At the next lower levels, policies may further define unethical and imprudent behavior as well as specific assets to be protected. And policies should specifically forewarn employees of the consequences of prohibited acts.

This means written ethics policies and codes of conduct that discourage and deter unethical and illegal behavior. The codes should be distributed to management and employees and contain specific prohibitions that may include theft, embezzlement, fraud, destruction of company property, falsifying attendance, payroll, production and expense reports, gambling on company time and property, sexual harassment, and any other examples that might apply.

Controlling unethical conduct in organizations is largely a matter first of all of role modeling. If executives and supervisors behave ethically, employees tend to conform to an ethical standard. After role modeling, the next best defense is the establishment of a corporate code of ethics and an anticrime policy. Written codes of conduct, adopted and adhered to by top management, can have a positive effect in deterring unlawful behavior in the organization. But the establishment of the code isn't the end of the problem. The code must be enforced. So third of all, enforcement procedures should also be spelled out so that violations get reported, investigated, and disposed of.

In attempting to reduce theft, fraud, and embezzlement, an important task of management is to communicate clearly to employees that theft is considered to be and will be treated as a serious problem. The major consequence of a theft policy is that it conveys to employees the organization's concern for theft. Corporate officials must unambiguously communicate that theft of company property will invoke sanctions on the employee who steals.

## Employee Loyalty Cannot Be Bought, But It Can Be Earned _____

When we sign on with a new employer, there is more than one contract of employment. There is a formal contract that sets forth the general terms and conditions of employment. There is also a nonverbalized psychological contract that covers such things as the new employee's depth of commitment (loyalty) to the company. In exchange for that commitment, however, the new employee expects certain noneconomic rewards from the company. For example, the new employee expects and hopes the employer will provide a modest amount of employment security (stable employment). The new employee will also hope and expect to be treated with civility and fairness by the employer and to develop and cultivate good working relationships with coworkers. If those expectations are realized on the job, the employee will experience a high level of job satisfaction and will perform at a high level.

If the company fails to meet the terms of this psychological contract, the employee will feel a low level of satisfaction, perform poorly, and become a candidate for termination. So there is a quid pro quo (some benefit for each party) in the psychological contract. It is not one-sided. In that sense, company loyalty is a two-way street, with rights and obligations on both parties.

## Workplace Privacy and Policy Issues _____

Management should always be aware of workplace privacy issues. Policies must cover inspections and searches of company equipment and facilities used by employees; employee surveillance; investigative interviews and reports; and disciplinary measures. Each of these areas is a legal trap that could lead to charges of malicious prosecution, invasion of privacy, defamation, false imprisonment, or infliction of emotional distress.

### Employee Privacy vs. the Protection of Assets

Throughout the workplace experience, there are broad areas of privacy contention. These include the use of employee screening and monitoring information from: arrest/criminal records; financial (checking account, investments, loans); credit information reporting; medical records; employment records; education records; investigative agencies/background investigations; psychological tests; personal identification/verification methods; "service monitoring" methods or equipment; electronic surveillance equipment; investigative files or dossiers; internal control, detection, access control procedures or equipment; and the employee personnel file.

While the organization must deal with the presence of an expectation of privacy, it should promulgate a clear statement on privacy designed to temper an employee expectation of privacy and assert employer ownership, authority, and oversight of the facility, equipment, and supplies. Employee usage of computer equipment, for example, is at the employer's discretion. The employee uses the computer with rules and restrictions that are designed to protect the employer's property and serve legitimate business interests, such as the employer's need to keep books of account or invoice customers.

Policies, rules, and actions should clarify that individual access to the facility, an interior area, or a specific piece of equipment, such as a computer, is via an access control device or system controlled and administered by company security or network administrators.

## Embezzlement Policy Considerations _____

Keep in mind the following:

1. The outline of any policy may be reviewed or entirely written by legal counsel. Certainly, the final draft should be reviewed and approved by the responsible company officer and counsel.
2. This policy will be reviewed periodically and updated in light of new legal developments and corporate experiences.
3. The policy is not an employment contract.

### Prohibited Conduct

1. The policy should include a clear statement forbidding embezzlement, larceny, misappropriation, willful misapplication, or other illegal actions against and affecting fixed or liquid company assets.

2. It should also cover misuse of the company's internal corporate accounting system and other related systems and equipment to carry out any of the above illegal acts.

## Promulgation of the Policy

The policy should be:

1. Disseminated to all those whose conduct it is to govern.
2. Written clearly, easily understood.
3. Include a space for recipient sign-off with initials and date.
4. Communicated in one of three ways, via employee handbook (maintain a log of employees who receive the handbook); posting on employee bulletin boards; or through physical distribution of the printed text.

## Reporting Systems

The company should create and publicize a reporting system for reporting criminal conduct within the organization and that allows employees to do so without fear of retribution. There are several ways to handle this requirement. A policy directive from corporate management should first clarify when to report a possible embezzlement, under what circumstances, and to whom. Additionally, policy statements should state that suspected wrongdoing will be investigated thoroughly, and that suspects will be treated fairly and consistently without regard to position within the company or length of service.

### Reporting System: Fraud Hotlines

The company may want to create and publicize a mechanism for reporting criminal conduct within the organization and that allows employees to do so without fear of retribution. There are several ways to handle this requirement. The earlier policy directive from corporate management should clarify when to report criminal conduct, under what circumstances, and to whom.

A fraud hotline is a mechanism that has been used in government and business. The major elements that have been found necessary for a successful hotline are:

- A clear statement of the hotline's mission and objectives;
- Staff with interview skills and compliance program knowledge;
- Controls to protect the confidentiality of callers;
- Internal guidelines to evaluate and classify allegations received through calls or letters;
- Policy that inquiries into the allegations are performed by independent and qualified personnel;
- Procedures to monitor cases to assure they are being handled and resolved properly.

## Investigative Responses

Once an offense has been discovered, though not fully verified, the company must take all reasonable steps to respond appropriately to the offense. This means the company must conduct an internal investigation of the incident and complete it within in a reasonable period of time. Responsibility for conducting an investigation should be stated, whether it is assigned to internal auditing, security, legal counsel, or outside investigators. An incident need not be reported to any appropriate governmental authorities if the company concludes, based on the information then available, that no criminal or compliance-related offense had been committed. The company should have in place a systematic records and document retention and destruction program designed to be effective in meeting the legitimate business needs and legal obligations, including internal investigations, of the corporation.

If a criminal act is uncovered the company will report to and cooperate with law enforcement; investigative results will also be reported to the audit committee. The company may report an incident to the bonding company as required under an insurance policy.

## Violations and Enforcement of Policy

### Enforcement and Sanctions

The following guidelines apply:

1. They must be consistent in application.
2. They must include disciplinary mechanisms for three types of violations: (1) illegal conduct, (2) unethical conduct, and (3) failure to detect an offense.
3. They must define conduct that is grounds for termination.
4. Disciplinary measures should not conflict with employment laws or union rules.
5. Disciplinary measures will apply to supervisors, managers, and executives who condone questionable, improper, or illegal conduct by those reporting to them or who fail to take appropriate corrective action when such matters are brought to their attention.
6. Termination action should not conflict with the personnel manual; the policy should spell out precisely what the company would do to an employee caught embezzling or stealing company property (consult with legal counsel on termination action).
7. The legal department shall report periodically to management and the audit committee each confirmed violation of this policy of which it has knowledge.

If the company antiembezzlement policy has an immediate termination/no exceptions clause, the company should be prepared to defend it. While such a clause may be consistent, most companies prefer a two- or three-stage procedure, moving into a disciplinary policy of warning, counseling/reminder of the policy, and then termination or prosecution. An alternative clause could read, "Violation of corporate policies by employees will invoke disciplinary measures up to and including termination."

Company policy concerning prosecution should always be clearly stated and be in the name of the CEO. The prosecution policy should include a requirement that anticipated prosecutive actions be reviewed with legal counsel prior to their initiation.

## Communicating Policy Requirements

There must be effective communication of company ethics policies and codes of conduct to all employees and agents. This may be done by requiring participation in training programs or by disseminating publications that will effectively communicate to employees how to prevent and detect wrongdoing. "Effective" means explaining in plain English what is required. The communications must also be specific, relevant to the wrongdoing to be avoided, and directed to those who may be in a position to violate the law.

The form or medium for communications and training is left to the company. All that matters is that the materials educate and inform employees about their ethical and legal responsibilities. In short, if it works, use it. But be prepared to prove that it works.

One way to look at implementing communication requirements is to create programs for three levels of officers and personnel in the organization. For example:

- Level 1: Board members, audit committee, CEO and executive level managers cover fundamentals of a statute or a range of relevant statutes that could affect the company, such as those dealing with money laundering, fraudulent wire transfers, and so forth. They should examine, too, how to assess management compliance, and how to establish and monitor policy, internal controls, audits, and investigations. Also of concern would be the possibility of various forms of negligence, such as vicarious or derivative liability, willful organizational indifference, or the responsible corporate officer doctrine.
- Level 2. Middle managers, supervisors, line managers, group leaders, and staff specialists cover legal matters in their particular areas, and offer guidance on how to recognize and report violations along with how to establish and monitor internal controls.
- Level 3. Frontline personnel use supervisors to give verbal descriptions and real-world, company/job-specific examples of prohibited behavior; use positive reinforcement for accepted behavior; and explain how to report violations to a supervisor or use a "reporting hotline."

Companies often have antitheft or embezzlement policies inserted in the employee handbook, and employees do a one-time sign-off on the entire handbook. However, the courts are moving in the direction of having company rules and policies clearly and repeatedly communicated to employees and consistently applying those rules.

In addition to the considerations described above, give employees a legal definition of embezzlement. And, perhaps, add larceny, the wrongful taking and carrying away of the personal property of another with intent to convert it or deprive the owner of its use or possession, and explain the differences. Follow this up by real-world, company-related examples of the kind of behavior that is unlawful. Also define and give examples of behavior that is unethical and unacceptable to the company.

### Evaluating Compliance Communications

Suppose you've written a policy guide for your organization and had it disseminated to managers and employees. Did everyone understand it? How can you prove that they did? Well, you could use a sort of fog index before the policy was disseminated. Or, you could use a sign-off, requiring employees to say they understood the policy. Or you could get a team of interviewers to test the comprehension and understanding of the policy among employees on a random or statistical basis. Again, the point is that your organization must show the effectiveness of its compliance communications.

## Conclusion

Communications is at the core of an effective policy or code of conduct. Without it, a policy is meaningless, and worse, will not pass legal scrutiny. A program must be ongoing, reflecting changes in a company's perceived risks, and responding to new legal and regulatory mandates. Communications must respond and follow these changes and always maintain a strategy of testing and proving that the message is getting through to the personnel it is supposed to affect.

## Audits of Policy Compliance

The purpose of these is to monitor compliance with policy directives and procedures.

Those performing them should:

1. Set frequency and timing of audits.
2. Make sure that they are conducted by the internal audit department.
3. Focus on formal and informal management controls and assess effectiveness.
4. Provide a thorough review of all controls in each area.
5. Document and report findings to the audit committee of the board of directors.

# *Vulnerability Assessments*

Vulnerability assessments are the method for determining the relative potential for loss of specific assets in a program or function. A vulnerability assessment consists of the following steps:

1. Analysis of the control environment
2. Analysis of the inherent risk
3. Preliminary evaluation of security and safeguards

The auditor must decide if controls are adequate, if they work, and if they are reasonable. Are there gaping holes in the control structure, or does it look tight? The auditor's reliance on an organization's internal control structure, without a thorough examination, often makes the discovery of fraud more difficult.

## Principles of Controls

A "control" is any device, action, or procedure that reduces the likelihood that an exposure to the risk of asset loss will occur. Almost all fraud and embezzlements have occurred because specific controls were compromised, either intentionally or accidentally, or their warning was ignored by management.

As an example, validity checks are designed to:

1. Separate duties between those with property handling responsibilities and those with property recording responsibilities.

2. Determine that (1) a purchase has been approved by someone with authority to commit funds for such purposes, (2) from a vendor who is approved, (3) by a person who is authorized to buy, (4) that the specific goods ordered were in fact received, and (5) that the unit price charged and extensions are stated correctly on the vendor's invoice.

3. Provide an oversight mechanism at each step in the processing of transactions that detects errors, omissions, and improprieties in the previous step. (Division of labor and dual responsibility for related transactions, by means of a counter-signature, the segregation of functions, or dollar authorization limits, for example forces collusion by at least two parties to effect a fraudulent transaction.)

Validity checks involve authorization procedures established to determine whether a payment to be made is based on a legitimate claim against the company by a vendor or supplier who has in fact supplied something of corresponding value.

## Security Vulnerabilities and Control Issues

- Security of check stock, signature stamps, and check imprinting equipment.
- Secure storage locations for cash, securities, bonds, and other financial instruments.
- Encoding of company checks with information on operator, date of printing, and serial number.
- Physical security features in checks, such as watermarks, security inks, chemical voids, reflective holograms, high-resolution microprinting, void pantographs, bar coding, glyphs, and perforators.
- Secure storage for removable files and fonts.
- Bank provided with a daily list of checks written on the account; this is matched by bank and verified by customer.
- Accounting, bookkeeping, and key personnel are secured with a fidelity bond.
- All blank checks and signature stamps are physically secured.
- All cash, securities, and other financial instruments are stored in a physically secured area or safe or vault.
- All blank invoices, purchase order forms, and credit memos are physically secured.
- The purchasing department is separated from receiving responsibilities; the supervisor is not authorized to pay bills.
- Approval for payment is given only when the related purchase order and receiving copy are attached.
- The purchasing department uses prenumbered orders for all purchases; copies go to receiving and accounting.
- Cash or credit returns are supervised by two persons.
- The purchasing department is periodically audited.

- Payroll checks are not signed by the person who prepared the payroll.
- The amounts paid are confirmed with the payroll records.
- Signature endorsements on cashed checks are compared with signatures on employment records.
- Work orders, rates paid for overtime and temporary or part-time help are reviewed frequently.
- All canceled and unclaimed checks are accounted for and secured.
- The computer operator/bookkeeper does not handle cash, open incoming mail, mail statements, do follow-ups on delinquent receivables, approve write-offs of bad accounts, or approve refunds or credits.
- The cutoff bank statement is used to audit the cash account; this is done periodically and on a surprise basis.
- Bank reconciliations are performed, reviewed, and verified each month.
- Blank checks are never signed.
- Checks are never signed without supporting documentation (such as purchase orders, payroll forms, invoices).

## Electronic Commerce

Problems can occur in the following situations:

- Lack of authentication of transaction authorization.
- Interception of data by outsiders.
- Lack of physical access control to computer system.
- Inadequate and weak access control system.
- Introduction of computer viruses to networked systems.
- Inadequate control over storage media.
- Single user in a microcomputer system authorizes and records transactions.
- Check management software that specifies limits to dollar amounts of signatures. Management awareness and support of computer security measures is low or absent.
- Users have the ability to enter a range of specific database choices.
- Sensitive fields are available on data entry screens.
- Users may download accounting information to personal computers.
- Critical computer file backup procedures are not enforced.
- Multilevel password control systems are not in use.
- Password-controlled disk lock system is not used.
- Networks are not protected by any type of firewall (screening routers, operating system or application-based system).
- Cryptography is not used in either computer communications or storage systems.

# Chapter 11

# Internal Controls

Organizations face new responsibilities for protecting assets and for reporting on the effectiveness of internal controls. In addition, it is critical that the relationship between internal controls, compliance programs, and possible illegal acts be fully understood. As described below, internal controls are required for effective compliance programs and for protecting an organization's financial, physical, and intellectual assets. Some key guidance, however, is found in the following laws and auditing literature.

## A Comprehensive Description of Internal Controls

A report entitled "Internal Control—Integrated Framework," issued in 1992 by the Committee of Sponsoring Organizations (COSO)* developed integrated guidance on internal control. The guidance provided in this report is designed to give a common definition of internal control and establish a standard by which companies can assess their system of internal control.

Every business decision involves judgment and chance. And every system of internal control has its limitations, as described in the report. As such, fraudulent financial reporting and accounting surprises can never be eliminated totally. However, it is COSO's view that if management, boards of directors, external auditors, and others adopt the components, criteria, and guidelines set forth in the report, the incidence of such events will be reduced.

---

*COSO members include the following organizations: the American Institute of Certified Public Accountants, the American Accounting Association, the National Association for Accountants, the Institute of Internal Auditors, and the Financial Executives Institute.

The COSO report tries to settle on a definition of internal control in the hope that laws and regulations will adopt an agreed-upon nomenclature. The study defines internal control as a process, "effected by an entity's board of directors, management, and other personnel, designed to provide reasonable assurance regarding the achievement of objectives in the following categories:

- Effectiveness and efficiency of operations.
- Reliability of financial reporting.
- Compliance with applicable laws and regulations."

The study points out that there are five interrelated components of internal control that must be present and functioning to have an effective control system. These components are:

Control environment: the integrity, ethical values, and competence of the entity's people; management's philosophy and operating style; the way management assigns authority and responsibility, and organizes and develops its people; and the attention and direction provided by the board of directors.

Risk assessment: the identification and analysis of relevant risks as they influence achievement of the objectives, forming a basis for determining how risks should be managed.

Control activities: the policies and procedures that help ensure management directives are carried out. They include a range of activities as diverse as approvals, authorizations, verifications, reconciliations, reviews of operating performance, security of assets, and segregation of duties.

Information and communication: generated data as well as information about external events, plus clear messages from top management that control responsibilities must be taken seriously.

Monitoring: a process that assesses the quality of the system's performance over time.

Internal controls, according to the report, can help an entity achieve its performance and profitability targets, prevent loss of resources, and ensure reliable financial reporting.

Roles and responsibilities for internal controls are spelled out in the report. While everyone has responsibility for internal controls, "the chief executive officer is ultimately responsible and should assume 'ownership' of the system...Management is accountable to the board of directors, which provides governance, guidance and oversight...Internal auditors evaluate the effectiveness of control systems, and contribute to ongoing effectiveness."

## The Foreign Corrupt Practices Act's Internal Accounting Control Standards

When the Foreign Corrupt Practices Act (FCPA) was enacted in 1977, the emphasis was on preventing corrupt payments to foreign officials. The law's antibribery section prohibits SEC-registered American businesses from certain corrupt practices in dealing with foreign officials. To determine if any bribery payments were made and to prevent companies from hiding them, the law imposes certain record-keeping and internal control standards. These "accounting standards" require affected companies to:

- Make and keep books, records, and accounts, which, in reasonable detail, accurately and fairly reflect the transactions and disposition of the assets of the issuer; and

- Devise and maintain a system of internal accounting controls sufficient to provide reasonable assurance that 1) transactions are executed in accordance with management's general or specific authorizations; 2) transactions are recorded as necessary to permit preparation of financial statements in conformity with generally accepted accounting principals or any other criteria applicable to such statements; and 3) access to assets is permitted only in accordance with management's general or specific authorizations; and 4) the recorded accountability for assets is compared with the existing assets at reasonable intervals, and appropriate action is taken with respect to any difference.

The FCPA has been used to prosecute domestic and foreign violations. The accounting standards section has become the most significant part of the FCPA because it makes it a criminal offense not to maintain accurate books and records and systems of internal controls.

## U.S. Sentencing Commission Guidelines Mandate Controls and Monitoring

Under the federal sentencing guidelines, organizations can get reduced sanctions for having internal controls that will reasonably assure the detection of criminal conduct by their employees and agents. The organization must take reasonable steps through controls and auditing systems that will detect and prevent loss of assets. The guidelines seem to be calling for a full range of controls, far beyond those normally required to prevent accounting irregularities.

The organization must also take reasonable steps through monitoring and auditing systems that will detect criminal conduct by its employees and agents. The guidelines imply that an organization have accounting and systems controls that would detect and deter waste, fraud, and abuse of assets, plus informal mechanisms related to organizational structure and management controls. In decentralized companies, branches and subsidiaries would need similar controls and audits.

## Banking Law Requires Internal Controls

The Federal Deposit Insurance Corporation (FDIC) Improvement Act of 1991 requires issuance of an annual report by the largest depository institutions, signed off by management and an independent public accountant, on internal controls over financial reporting. The CEO, chief accountant, internal auditor, or financial officer must sign a report stating management's responsibilities for preparing financial statements, and for establishing a yearly assessment of "the effectiveness of such internal control structures and procedures."

## Securities Litigation Reform Law

The 1995 Private Securities Litigation Reform Act (U.S. Public Law 104–67) amends the Securities and Exchange Act of 1934 (15 USCS 78a et seq.) and requires auditors to design audit procedures that will likely detect illegal acts that would have "a direct and material effect" on a publicly held company's financial statement.

With computers often the main tool used to create results used in financial statements, auditors must look at computer safeguards and controls as well as the overall internal controls of a company. Auditors must also assess the risks and vulnerabilities of a company to fraud. If illegal acts are thought to be possible, or are discovered, these must be reported to top management or the audit committee. If the auditor's report does not receive timely action by management, the auditors must inform the Securities and Exchange Commission.

For each audit of an issuer's financial statement, the independent auditor must use "procedures designed to provide reasonable assurance of detecting illegal acts...that would have a direct and material effect on the determination of financial statement amounts." The act has some key words and phrases that should be examined. "Procedures designed to provide reasonable assurance of detecting..." can be interpreted to mean an evaluation of internal controls and risks to the specific assets of the firm. Absent from the Congressional reports on the Act was the term "internal accounting controls." The phrase "internal controls" has a far broader meaning and refers to management and administrative controls, security and safeguards, and monitoring in financial and operational areas. Thus any current audit of financial statements will encompass risks and vulnerabilities in all area of the firm. The use of "illegal acts" implies a broad range of frauds, including fraudulent reporting, kickbacks, bribery, money laundering, embezzlement, and intellectual property misuse.

## Definitions of Controls Get Clarification

The most important thing to keep in mind is that once vague definitions are now more concrete, and responsibilities have been clarified; this should lead to a common understanding among management, auditors, security, legal counsel, and regulators that:

1. Management is responsible for establishing internal controls that ensure the accurate reporting of financial information of their organization and the effectiveness of its internal control systems;
2. The function of the auditor is to examine and attest to the accuracy of the financial information. This has meant only things that could affect the accurate gathering, recording, and reporting of financial transactions. The expanded definition calls for examining internal controls that safeguard assets from losses that could have a material effect on the financial statement.
3. There are internal controls that apply to all companies and there are internal controls that cover all assets—financial, physical, and intellectual.
4. There is a set of criteria for evaluating risks to assets and establishing internal controls that are company-specific.

## Can Management Controls Become Too Much of a Good Thing? ____

Establishing effective and efficient management controls tends to be a matter of balancing costs against benefits. Tipping the balance to either extreme of over- or undercontrol is inefficient and ineffective. The cost of implementing controls is far easier to calculate than the intended benefits of such controls, because costs tend to be quantitative, while benefits tend to be qualitative. Deciding how much control should be exercised in any organization is not a simple matter. Furthermore, both economic and behavioral considerations include direct and consequential costs (acquisition costs and implementation and maintenance costs).

Behavioral considerations have to do with the impact controls may have on personal productivity. Do control costs impact on human performance and job satisfaction? Worse yet, do controls take on the aura of absolute rules, prohibitions, and mandatory actions and thus discourage judgment and discretion? Slavish compliance is required when controls are designed and enforced without rationality, without need, and without consideration for the sensitivities of the people affected by them. But they become more venerated in their violation than by their compliance. Covert and overt resistance can follow. In fact, in some organizational settings, overcontrol often results in petty acts of fraud and thievery, (such as lying on expense accounts and "fudging" performance data to name two methods of rebellion).

How can you overcome resistance to or negative reactions to controls? Make sure that goals, objectives, and control standards are realistic, not improbable or impossible to achieve. Standards, goals, and objectives should focus on the benefits of the change to the organization itself and its people.

## Internal Controls ____

Organizations face new responsibilities for protecting assets and for reporting on the effectiveness of internal controls. In addition, it is critical that the relationship between internal controls and compliance programs communicate the reasons for the change—cost savings, theft reduction, loss prevention, prudence, regulatory requirement, and so on. Relate the new controls to meaningful and accepted corporate goals.

Do *not* overcontrol. The costs always outweigh the benefits when you overcontrol.

## Seven Common Inadequacies in an Organization's Control Environment

1. Inadequate rewards for employee performance.
2. Insufficient internal controls—in particular, a lack of suitable separation of duties or audit trails.
3. Ambiguity in employee job roles, duties, responsibilities, and areas of accountability.
4. Failure to counsel employees and to take suitable administrative action when performance levels or personal behavior fall below acceptable levels.
5. Lack of timely periodic audits, inspections, and operational reviews and a failure of senior executives to follow up on their results to ensure that the

organization's goals, priorities, policies, and procedures—as well as relevant government regulations—are being complied with.

6. Insufficient orientation and training of employees and executives on legal, ethical, and security issues and the organization's policies for resolving them.

7. Inadequate organizational policies with respect to sanctions for legal, ethical, and security breaches and a failure of senior executives to monitor and enforce these policies.

## Basic Controls and Security

- Accounting, bookkeeping, and key personnel are secured with a fidelity bond.
- All blank checks and signature stamps are physically secured.
- All cash, securities, and other financial instruments are stored in a physically secured area or safe or vault.
- All blank invoices, purchase order forms, and credit memos are physically secured.
- The purchasing department is separated from receiving responsibilities; the supervisor is not authorized to pay bills.
- Approval for payment is given only when the related purchase order and receiving copy are attached.
- The purchasing department uses prenumbered orders for all purchases; copies go to receiving and accounting.
- Cash or credit returns are supervised by two persons.
- The purchasing department is periodically audited.
- Payroll checks are not signed by the person who prepared the payroll.
- The amounts paid are confirmed with the payroll records.
- Signature endorsements on cashed checks are compared with signatures on employment records.
- Work orders, rates paid for overtime and temporary or part-time help are reviewed frequently.
- All canceled and unclaimed checks are accounted for and secured.
- The computer operator/bookkeeper does not handle cash, open incoming mail, mail statements, do follow-ups on delinquent receivables, approve write-offs of bad accounts, or approve refunds or credits.
- The cutoff bank statement is used to audit the cash account; this is done periodically and on a surprise basis.
- Bank reconciliations are performed, reviewed, and verified each month.
- Blank checks are never signed.
- Checks are never signed without supporting documentation (such as purchase orders, payroll forms, invoices).

# Preventing On-the-Job Fraud, Theft, and Embezzlement

- Establish tight, but not oppressive or cost-inefficient internal controls. Monitor such controls for exceptions.
- Conduct follow-up audits of control exceptions, accounting errors, and irregularities.
- Take appropriate and timely administrative action when errors or irregularities are found.
- Establish an ethical code and an ethical work environment.
- Provide ethics training.
- Provide role models for ethical conduct from the senior management level on down.
- Hire honest people and keep them honest by providing a safe and secure work environment, and by producing fair rewards and recognition for good performance.
- Provide employees with opportunities for professional and personal growth and development.
- Provide employees with adequate resources, training and support to get the job done right—the first time.

## Basic Financial Controls for the Professional Office or Small Business

Remember, anyone is capable of committing embezzlement or fraud. To discourage such crimes from happening, you should establish, monitor, and enforce the following internal controls:

- Bookkeeper, office manager or accountant, and key personnel are secured with a fidelity bond.
- Separate duties; no one person should control an entire financial transaction.
- All blank checks and signature stamps should be physically secured.
- Only the owner or senior officer should sign company checks.
- Verify all documents in any transaction of goods or money before signing.
- Monitor cash receipts, that the cash deposited reflects the actual cash intake.
- Total invoices, check the amount posted, reconcile with the amount deposited.
- Have bank statements sent to the owner's home or delivered by courier only to you.
- Reconcile bank statements: match bank statements with deposit slips and checks; check the amount, payee and signature on each check.

# Controlling Access to Computers and Networks

Access control is a process by which an individual is allowed or denied access to a specific facility or interior area or object, such as a computer, or its software applications, or to communications networks. The basis of access control is identifying a person seeking access. Physical security and access control are taking on greater importance in thwarting and detecting embezzlement by enforcing separation of duties and providing audit trails. Knowing the basics of access control will help you understand how the systems operate from building entry to communications networks.

Methods of identification usually include one or more of the following:

- Something a person has, such as a key, a card, a token or other artifact
- Something a person knows, such as a password, a code or a combination of word, phrase, and number
- Something a person is, an unalterable personal characteristic or physical attribute such as fingerprints, voiceprint, or hand geometry
- Something a person does, such as handwriting or the pattern of keystroke entry

## Levels of Control

There are three general levels of access control. In the lowest level, there are locks and keys, code/combination locks, passwords, badges, and so forth. Advantages of these items are that they are usually inexpensive, easy to use, have employee acceptance, and require little training or judgment by security personnel. Disadvantages include their failure to provide positive identification/verification of authorized holder, not to mention the fact that the item or knowledge needed for access can be lost, stolen, or disclosed, or the item may even be counterfeited.

## Passwords

Passwords are the most common form of computer access control. A password can be very simple—a single letter or number—or complex—an algorithm based on date or time.

A password can be chosen by the computer user or assigned to the user. Often the problem with a user-chosen password is that it runs from the familiar and easy to the dumb. Here are a few examples: the name of a sports team, a pet, a friend, sexual terms, or words such as "secret," "enter," "payday," or any other name associated with ethnicity, the seasons, or the company.

User-chosen passwords are usually "weak," that is, easy to guess or reveal through a dictionary or password-cracking software. For example, a password should not be a simple word or combination of words; one's birthday or that of a spouse or family member; or a series of numbers or letters. Yet people will naturally pick a word or phrase that is familiar and easy to remember.

A strong password should have a minimum length (six to eight characters) and contain both alphabetic and numeric characters. One way would be to choose random characters that are easy to remember but difficult to guess. Another is to choose answers to a set of rotating specific questions drawn from highly personal knowledge, opinions, or interests. A drawback to assigned passwords is that they are often too difficult to remember, and people then tend to write them down so they won't forget them.

## Password Security Checklist

__ There should be written policy and procedures on selecting and disclosing passwords.

__ Passwords should be kept secret and known only to the user.

__ Passwords should not be displayed near or on the user's computer.

__ Passwords should be difficult to guess, and easy to remember, and have a minimum length as well as alphabetic and numeric characters.

__ System-assigned/generated passwords are usually preferred.

__ Passwords should be encrypted when kept in the computer system.

__ Passwords should be changed regularly: monthly, every 60 days or every three months if user-selected; every six months is an option for system-generated passwords, but no longer than once a year for any password.

__ Passwords and other access codes should be deactivated immediately when an employee leaves the company.

__ A periodic audit should be performed to determine if the company's password security policies and procedures are being followed and are still effective.

## Second-Level Access Control Systems

At the next level, there are various ID cards, photo badges, personal recognition by a guard or other authorized person, and combinations or two-level systems requiring say, a coded card and cipher or digital/keypad entry system. The advantages of these systems is that they are only moderately expensive, and that compromise of the system is more difficult because two items of identification are required. Magnetic-stripe cards are part of an established, low-cost, secure, reliable, efficient, and world-wide accepted system. Advances in magnetic-stripe technology have allowed a number of combinations such digitized personal biometric attributes.

Disadvantages, however, are that counterfeiting or impersonation is possible, and reliance on judgment of security personnel may be too great.

Non-repetitive systems, one-time passwords, and using random pass-code generation with a keypad or hand-held decoders, offer increased security in that there is no pattern to the authentication that can be copied.

### Smart Cards and Portable Data Carriers

A smart card functions as a portable database, a computer in a credit-card-size package. Its most common form is that of a standard credit card, but it can also be configured like a personal identification badge or any other shape required. The card allows information to be accessed and retrieved via a card reader connected to a personal computer, terminal, automatic teller machine, point-of-sale terminal, telephone, electronic lock or any number of other devices.

Software resides within the reader and is also located on the card in the form of integrated circuits. The function of the reader is to detect the presence of a card and to provide a standard interface so that the card can communicate with different hosts.

Host computers or terminals can interact with the smart card, which simplifies the design of the application. Because of the flexibility of this special operating system, the card's data files can be partitioned, supporting multiple independent applications on one card.

Security, such as a multiple-level, hierarchical structure guarded by a password and/or personal identification number (PIN), bar code, or a biometric ID, can be built in. Each data file stored in the card can be assigned its own security level, with separate read and write permissions. Passwords can be self-selected or assigned by a system administrator.

The cost of installing smart card readers and retrofitting existing systems to handle smart cards is very high, which has slowed broad adoption. However, smart card technology is becoming standardized; they are multi-technology cards providing access control IDs for computer and database access, and digital and cellular communications. They also provide authentication and encryption as well as carry decryption keys. Smart cards are carrying chips with faster processors and bigger read-only memories, and are becoming easier to use with smaller or radio frequency (RF) readers.

## Top-Level Control Systems

At the highest level, there are the biometric systems, which have the following advantage: It is very difficult and costly to forge or counterfeit an individual's unique physical characteristics, so the deterrent effect is very high. Disadvantages include costs that are higher than most other security devices and enrollment and access times that may be higher than for other systems.

We will turn our focus to the last two methods of identification, something a person is or does. This area is usually called biometric identification, and it is the security technique that holds the most promise for positive personal identification for access control. We will look at the basic technologies of biometrics, the security applications, the major product vendors, and possible new developments in biometrics.

### Biometric Security Systems

Biometrics in security is the machine/computer identification and verification of persons based on biological or physiological measurements. In general operation, the system consists of a device that scans or replicates the characteristic to be measured. That is, the device may record a series of words or a photograph, or laser scan a fingerprint or an eye's vessel pattern; or it may measure the length of a person's fingers and the spread of the hand, the speed, pressure and size of a person's signature, or the speed and rhythm of keystrokes in data entry. The computer and appropriate software store, process, and analyze the measurements.

For securing access to a computer, a database, or a network, a system based on positive identification of the user would be desirable. A positive ID system would provide an accurate and legally convincing audit trail for financial/information transactions or for investigations of computer-related fraud.

The major biometric security systems in use today and how they operate are described below.

Facial scanning, also called facial thermogram or mapping, relies on an algorithm for pattern recognition unique to an individual's face. For access control, a small video camera is connected to a computer, the person seeking access looks into the camera, and the scanning verifies or rejects the person depending on the scanning match.

In a computer terminal access application, a camera can continuously view the terminal user and confirm that person's identity. If the authorized user leaves or another sits down at the terminal, the security system's facial recognition algorithm can trigger a sign-off by the original terminal user and require a sign-on by the new user before that person can begin using the terminal.

Fingerprints: a computerized system uses electro-optical recognition and file matching of fingerprint minutiae.

Fingertips: algorithms are derived from measurements of the individual's fingertip shape and texture.

Hand geometry: an electronic scan of a person's hand is made first. Ninety different aspects of the hand are measured and compared to a previous scan of the person, which provided a reference profile. This encoded profile data is stored either in computer memory or on a magnetic stripe or in a smart card. A positive match between the current hand scan and stored data allows access.

Iris recognition: the iris is the colored ring around the pupil of the eye. A scanning device measures and analyzes the unique color patterns of the iris, and takes a video picture of the iris, which is converted into a digital code that can be compared.

Keystroke dynamics: measures the speed and pattern of keystroke entry of an individual.

Retinal patterns: this system recognizes an individual by the retinal vessel pattern of the eye. A scanned reference picture is stored in a computer as a standard for comparison and matching.

Signature dynamics: automated signature verification systems are based on the dynamics of the signer's pen motion related to time. The measurements are signature shape, speed, stroke, pen pressure, and timing, taken via a digitized tablet. A signer is enrolled by taking three or more measurements of his signature; an average figure is obtained and stored in the computer. Future signatures are compared with the average figure.

Voice verification: "prints" of a person's voice are recorded in analog signal, which is converted to digital and a set of measurements are derived and stored in a computer. The references are based on an individual's vocal pattern obtained by having that person speak several words. The system may require an individual to say three words out of a reference file of seven, a match of the words spoken with those on file allows access.

## Access Control System Features: Physical Areas and Equipment ____

An analysis of access control requirements should begin with a physical security survey of the areas to be protected. Use a blueprint, layout, or drawing of the area to be surveyed and mark entry points and types of existing doors, closures, and locks. Also note any security or fire equipment already in place. This drawing can be used to analyze placement of access control units and perhaps tie in any security, safety, and fire detection equipment for monitoring on one system. Note also the traffic flow and patterns in the area during both normal working hours and off hours.

## Selecting an Access Control System

For the most part, today's biometric systems are compatible and integrate with access control systems that may be card-based. Therefore, when considering a biometric system, you should examine your current access control system and what you want to accomplish by adding or integrating a biometric system. Let's start with a review of basic system selection guidelines.

### General System Features

An access control system for a facility should have features and options that provide both sufficient capacity and flexibility to meet changing security needs. The following questions should be considered for basic features:

1. How many access points can be monitored?
2. How many cards, tokens, or readers can the system handle?
3. What access levels can be provided?
4. What types of access control devices can be integrated with the system?
5. Can secondary verification devices be added to the system in the future?
6. What time periods and personnel location parameters can be selected?
7. What types of reports can the system generate?
8. Are the readers vandal-resistant?
9. Can the system operate in a degraded mode?
10. Is there antipassback control?
11. Is there automatic door relock?
12. Is the system compatible with the existing computer and network?
13. Is the software documentation for the system complete and understandable?
14. Is there a start-up and ongoing training program for the access control system?
15. Is there a comprehensive maintenance agreement?
16. Will the vendor provide enhancements and, new releases, and at what cost?
17. Is the program source code available to do in-house enhancements?

## Prepare an Evaluation Table

Preparing a table to rate comparable access control systems can help your decision-making. With such a table you can rate types of systems or specific manufacturers. To set up a table, place the systems or brands of access control in a left-hand column. Put evaluation categories across the top of the table. The categories chosen, of course, will depend on what is most important and unique to your organization. Here are some basic categories to consider:

- Lowest procurement cost
- The costs of changing the ID, such as personal passwords, over a time period
- Lowest average monthly cost
- Best employee acceptance
- Best visitor acceptance
- Most compatible with security operations and personnel
- Ease of installation
- Ease of operation, including ID changes
- Most workable software
- Reliability of system operation
- Vendor warranty
- Technical training and support from vendor
- Highest level of security
- System preferred by insurance carrier

- System's ability to meet regulatory/legal/government contract requirements

## Selecting a Biometric System

In addition to some of the above items to consider, such as cost and user compatibility and acceptance, there are unique problems associated with selecting a biometric security system. Some basic questions you will have to ask vendors are:

1. How stable or reliable is the biometric attribute itself?
2. What can affect it (include the percentage of the population that lack the attribute, for instance, no fingers, can't speak, glaucoma sufferer)?
3. How accurate is the measurement of the biometric?
4. What is the system's storage capacity for biometric data?
5. What is the throughput or operating speed of the system?
6. What is the average enrollment time for users?
7. Is the system really needed? Is it too technical, too intrusive, too invasive, is there possible liability in making and storing biological details of a person, and what further "evidence" can be gleaned from biometric data?
8. How easy is it for the system to be "layered" with another biometric or ID?

The vendor should also supply information on error rates for false rejection of authorized personnel and false acceptance, or the admission of an impostor.

For high security, a very low false acceptance rate is important. Where authorized personnel should be allowed access with a minimum of inconvenience, a low false rejection rate is desirable. While equipment can be adjusted to modify error rates, one must always keep in mind the security objective for the specific access control point or object.

The vendor should also be able to supply information on lab tests of biometric systems; Sandia Labs, to name one, has performed tests for government agencies.

### Biometric Products and Vendors

A selection of current suppliers of biometric security systems and their products include:

- Facial recognition: Visionics Corp., Miros, NeuroMetric Vision Systems, Visage Technology
- Finger-image: Identicator Technology, Control Module, Unisys
- Fingerprint: Biometric Identification, Identix, AuthenTec, Biometric Identification, Digital Biometrics, Key Trak, NEC Technologies, Mytec Technologies
- Hand geometry: Recognition Systems, Konetix
- Iris recognition: IriScan, Sensar
- Key stroke dynamics: International Biometric Systems, which has come out with an inexpensive software package of its biometric system.
- Retinal scan: Eyedentify (based in Portland, Oregon)

- Signature dynamics: Digital Signature, CyberSign
- Voice verification: Thorn Automated Systems, Voice Sciences, Veritel, Keyware Technologies, Verbex Voice Systems and Kurzweil

## Possible Directions and Developments in Biometrics

In access control one can see total systems coming together—automated identification, data capture and storage, and data communications. Biometrics will be merged more with other access control IDs such as bar codes and magnetic-stripe and smart cards.

Biometrics used as a personal identifier may not be too far away. The hunt for a single identifier will be replaced by "layering" of, say, face and voice or fingerprint and signature. Identification technology and management is taking shape at the federal and state levels in tracking individuals at borders and airports, drivers licenses, secure patient records, benefits IDs, fraud control, and blood donors.

# *Chapter* *1 3*

# *Wire Transfer Embezzlements*

One method a company could use to gauge the potential severity of embezzlement loss is to determine the maximum amount of money that the accountant or a key financial officer of the company could move by wire transfer to another account. Most people tend to discount senior management when trying to determine the amount of loss that could occur. Even if top management were never to perpetrate an embezzlement, it is not inconceivable that someone could pretend to be a senior corporate officer and effect the wire transfer of funds to another account, where that money could be readily accessed by the embezzler.

Many companies lack adequate controls on wire transfers. There is a great dependence upon recognition of voices in arranging wire transfers, rather than the use of some other verification method.

## Legal Requirements of Fund Transfers

The Electronic Funds Transfer Act (EFTA) of 1978 (Title XX, 15 U.S.C. § 1693 et seq.) is the federal statute that covers a wide range of electronic funds transfers, including consumer payments.

Under the Bank Secrecy Act, and the amendments of the Annunzio-Wylie Anti-Money-Laundering Act of 1992, the Treasury and the Federal Reserve are authorized to require financial institutions to maintain records regarding domestic and international funds transfers. Such records are to be retained for five years. Wire transfers below $3,000 are exempted.

The originator's bank must retain, for each payment order accepted, the originator's name and address, the amount, the date, any payment instructions received with the payment order, the beneficiary bank identification, and if available, the beneficiary's name and address or account number.

For other than established customers, banks are to verify the name and address of the originator and the number of the verification document, which might be a driver's license, social security card, passport, or employer, taxpayer, or alien identification.

## Commercial Electronic Funds Transfers

The Uniform Commercial Code (UCC) sets rules and procedures that govern commercial transactions, including sales and payment methods, in most of the U.S. If any portion of a funds transfer is covered by the EFTA, the whole funds transfer is excluded from the Uniform Commercial Code Section 4A which covers commercial, bank-to-bank transactions. A section of the UCC, Article 4A, establishes standards and definitions for commercial wire transfers and defines the responsibilities of the parties involved. UCC Section 4A covers funds transfers involving one or more payment orders or credit transfers; a payment order may be transmitted by telephone, fax, telex, mail, or computer.

## Security Techniques and Procedures

The problems of authentication and verification of a payment order are covered under Section 4A-201, "Security Procedure." Security procedure is defined as "a procedure established by agreement of a customer and a receiving bank for the purpose of (i) verifying that a payment order is that of the customer, or (ii) detecting error in transmission or the content of the payment order or communication. A security procedure may require the use of algorithms or other codes, identifying words or numbers, encryption, callback procedures, or similar security devices."

A large percentage of payment orders and communications amending or canceling payment orders are transmitted electronically, and it is standard practice to use security procedures that are designed to assure the authenticity of the message. Security procedures can also be used to detect error in the content of messages or to detect payment orders that are transmitted by mistake, as in the case of multiple transmissions of the same payment order. Security procedures might also apply to communications that are transmitted by telephone or in writing. The definition of security procedure limits the term to a procedure "established by agreement of a customer and a receiving bank." The term does not apply to procedures that the receiving bank may follow unilaterally in processing payment orders. The question of whether loss that may result from the transmission of a spurious or erroneous payment order will be borne by the receiving bank or the purported sender is affected by whether a security procedure was or was not in effect and whether there was or was not compliance with the procedure.

Breaches of commercially reasonable security procedures, and attendant blame, "require that the person committing the fraud have knowledge of how the procedure works and knowledge of codes, identifying devices, and the like. That person may also need access to transmitting facilities through an access device or other software...This confidential information must be obtained either from a source controlled by the customer or from a source controlled by the receiving bank. The customer's responsibility is to supervise its employees to assure compliance with the security procedure and to safeguard confidential security information and access to transmitting facilities so that the security procedure cannot be breached."

If the customer can prove that the person committing the fraud did not obtain the confidential information from an agent or former agent of the customer or from a source controlled by the customer, the loss is shifted to the bank.

The customer, then, is not liable if it can prove that the bank or an outsider, such as a hacker, compromised its security.

## Unauthorized Payment Orders

Unauthorized payment orders are normally the responsibility of the customer in that "the customer has a duty to exercise ordinary care to determine that the order was unauthorized after it has received notification from the bank, and to advise the bank of the relevant facts within a reasonable time not exceeding 90 days after receipt of notification."

## Secure Online Consumer Payment Systems

Commerce on the Internet has spawned a number of different ways for consumers to order products and pay for them. With security perceived as a major problem in exposing credit card information, several systems have been proposed. More will come as the private sector leads the way in technology solutions to securing electronic transactions. One type of secure payment system takes the customer's financial information off-line, encrypts it and never displays it live on the Internet. The most common encryption method is the Data Encryption Standard (DES); another is public key encryption. Other software applications may use a Graphics User Interface (GUI) keypad, employing proprietary algorithms that randomly encrypt numbers, for example, those on a credit card, and send the numbers one at a time. Another method gives "digital certificates" to online banks, merchants, and consumers. The certificates can include Personal Identification Numbers (PINs), an authentication mechanism, and encryption.

## Secure Commercial Contracts

A security method for commercial and government contracts is the digital signature, defined in several state laws as an electronic identifier, created by a computer, and intended by the party using it to have the same force and effect as the use of a manual signature. While addressing transactions in state government only, when any written communication in which a signature is required or used, any party to the communication could affix a signature by use of a digital signature that complies with the requirements of a contract. The use of a digital signature may have the same force and effect as the use of a manual signature if it embodies all of the following attributes:

- It is unique to the person using it.
- It is capable of verification.
- It is under the sole control of the person using it.
- It is linked to data in such a manner that if the data are changed, the digital signature is invalidated.

## Network Access Control

Generally, network security has been designed to keep an unauthorized user from accessing the network, either externally or internally. The main technique has been a firewall, a security control gateway that channels communications and information.

A firewall seeks to control access to legitimate network users who have different authorization levels to applications and resources. For example, a firewall may insulate part of a network, a server, perhaps, that contains accounting and financial data.

# Accounting Information Systems: Access Control Checklists

## Personnel Access Control Matrix

Personnel should have access only to those areas and programs needed to perform their designated job. To help determine who may access what or be where, and when and under which set of conditions, devise an access control matrix. The left side column should list personnel by name or title; across the top line give the area or program; times or conditions of access can be given letter or numeral designations. A similar matrix can be designed for setting access controls for types of equipment, storage media, or network systems.

## Accounting Personnel Profiles

### Manager

\_\_\_ Does the manager of the computerized accounting system have experience in setting up a new set of books?

\_\_\_ Years of bookkeeping experience.

\_\_\_ Years of accounting experience.

\_\_\_ Years of computer training and experience.

Knowledge of:

Operating system_____

Finance/accounting programs_____

Database programs_____

Spreadsheets_____

Word processing_____

## Accounting Information Access Control Procedures _____

Accounting program controls should be able to:

- Restrict users to specific directories, programs, menu choices, and data files;
- Deny permission to copy specific documents, to transfer data onto disks, or to send out restricted information via e-mail or other electronic transfer;
- Create authorization tables that can limit user access to read-only, data input, data modification, and data deletion capabilities.

The accounting software should also provide: information/file masking, change-detection, audit trails; intrusion detection/alarm; recovery from network or database crashes; multi-level user rights for menus, forms, queries, and reports; file encryption; and database logs.

Accounting software should be evaluated for security in terms of how well it can enforce a segregation of duties that will deny or flag, for example, unauthorized changes to: finance charges, check formatting, invoices and statements, job costing, shipping and billing documentation, or sick time or vacation accruals.

For the accounting program modules given below, list who must have access and why, and the type or level of identification/verification required. This exercise is similar to devising the physical access control matrix.

- General ledger:
- Accounts receivable:
- Order entry and invoicing:
- Accounts payable:
- Check formatting and writing:
- Financial analysis:
- Payroll:
- Job costing:
- Inventory:
- Spreadsheet:
- Word processing:
- Database:

## Computer Access Controls _____

1. Are standard log-on procedures enforced?
2. Does someone have administrative responsibility for access authorization?
3. Are system stored passwords and codes encrypted?
4. Are all accesses logged?
- Is the date/time of access logged?

- Is establishment of authorizations by levels of authority or by levels of security?
- Are the functions performed identified?
- Is the computer or terminal identified?
- Are security violations logged?

5. Are there exceptions logging systems that will detect:
- Out of sequence, out of priority, and aborted runs and entries?
- Out of pattern transactions: too high, too low, too many, too often, too few, unusual file access (at odd times and from odd places)?
- Attempted access beyond authorization level?
- Repeated attempts to gain access improperly, with, for example, the wrong password or entry code?
- Parity and redundancy checks?

6. Are terminated employees' passwords or access code privileges canceled immediately?
7. Does the user/operator have restricted access to all programs and data files in the mainframe or network server(s)?
8. Are critical or sensitive data files protected from unauthorized access?
9. Are critical or sensitive data files protected from unauthorized update?
10. Are there any operating or processing controls that can detect fraudulent manipulation of data?
- Does software have change controllers, which limit access to critical or specified files?
- Do edit programs bar mainframe data that has been changed?
- Are data tagged with time and date of creation code?
- Is simultaneous access to a file or data field barred?
- Does the software provide an audit trail?

11. Does the operator maintain a record of what jobs are processed?
12. Are daily transactions summarized?
13. Are master files balances summarized?
14. Are exception reports generated?
15. Is there a transaction log?
16. Is the computer network protected by firewalls or other technology to control access?
17. Are there established and enforced secure procedures on how wire funds transfers are initiated and payment orders authorized?
18. Is a designated person allowed to send a funds transfer?
19. Are there identification and verification methods for the sender and the payment order?
20. Do wire transfer security measures include:
- Imposing limits on the amount of any transfer?

- Transfers payable only from an authorized account?
- Prohibiting any transfer that exceeds specific credit limits or account balances?
- Limiting transfer to authorized beneficiaries?

## Access Control Physical Security Survey

Regarding data processing areas/rooms/equipment (containing mainframe, PCs, network servers, or data media storage):

1. What hours do the computer areas operate? How many days per week?
2. Are employees who are authorized to enter data processing areas required to use a company-issued personal identification device? Is positive ID required for all vendors or consultants entering the computer or communications areas?
3. Are all other employees prohibited from freely entering computer areas?
4. Are signs posted on all entry doors prohibiting all non-authorized persons from entering? Is there a security log for visitors and employees?
5. Are guards or data processing supervisors positioned to observe any unauthorized entrant?
6. Under what conditions, if any, are nonauthorized persons given access to data processing areas?
   - Are they then under constant observation?
7. Is an access log kept of all persons who enter the data processing area?
8. Are storage media disks marked with a company logo or other identifiers?
9. Are company storage media leaving the facility subject to search and examination, including contents?

## Physical Security

1. Is there an access control and physical security system?
2. Is the system totally functional?
3. Are personal computers, lap- and palmtops, and notebooks secured with an alarm system, lock-down bars, cables, chains, fasteners, or other physical security devices?
4. Are disk drives secured with key locks?

## Data Backup and Security

1. Are sensitive/vital software and documentation, including payroll records, personnel records, and accounts receivable information secure?
2. Is a backup file kept at a secondary site? If so, are there any controls?
3. Do data backup and records retention and maintenance follow either laws or company policy?
4. Is there a thorough, appropriate, and tested disaster recovery plan?
5. Are restart procedures fully documented?

# Auditing for Fraud and Embezzlement

## Financial Versus Fraud Auditing

In conducting a financial audit for certification purposes, public accountants are alert to signs or evidence of errors and irregularities of a material nature. (The word "material" is used here in the context of a substantial amount.) Small errors or irregularities are of less concern to financial auditors.

On the other hand, fraud auditors or forensic accountants are very much concerned about small errors and irregularities if they seem to be related to the modus operandi of corrupt employees or employee thieves, embezzlers, and defrauders.

Small errors and irregularities may be the tip of a fraudulent iceberg. Criminals usually cannot bury all their tracks. Some part of their frauds, thefts, and embezzlements remain visible to the trained eye. Fraud auditors are trained by others or train themselves to be alert to such signs.

What kinds of small errors or irregularities do fraud auditors search for? They look for evidence of control procedure exceptions, accounting classification anomalies, oddities in financial trends, and ratios and oddities in specific transactions (too high, too low, too often, too rare, odd times, odd people, odd places, and so on). Fraud auditors also look for evidence of unexplained gaps or missing links in transaction processing times, places, and people and for misplaced or replaced transaction documentation.

In essence, financial auditors take a macro look at books, records, and controls, and fraud auditors take a micro look. Financial auditors see the big picture. Fraud auditors see the little picture.

## Audits of Manual and Computerized Systems

In a manual system, the audit trail is made up of paper documents that support each step in a regular business transaction (purchase or sale of goods or services), spanning from requisition, to purchase, to receipt of goods, and to payment, or from billing a customer, to receipt of his payment on account, and to its deposit in the bank. These paper documents are date and time stamped, and calculations are proofed and approved by supervisors and authorized for processing in the next step of the transaction. Copies of the documents are kept and filed at each step in the transaction. The audit trail in a manual system is therefore quite visible.

In computerized systems, particularly in online systems, the audit trail is somewhat invisible. Authorization of a transaction or a processing step may consist of a supervisor turning on a computer terminal key or an entry clerk entering a password or code at the terminal. Signatures, time stamps, and initials no longer exist on source documents to prove authorization.

In a manual system, paperwork accompanies a transaction from its point of origin to its end point. The paperwork literally travels with the product. In online systems, the system itself moves the product to its end point, with very little human intervention.

In a nutshell, an auditor in an online environment tends to audit systems and applications programs and their documentation much more than he tests individual transactions by flow of paperwork. The procedures reviewed in these audits are more often data entry procedures and file retention procedures than they are an examination of how documents are physically prepared, handled, and stored.

The documentation required in computerized accounting systems includes operator instructions, systems and program flowcharts, sample layouts for input and output records, program listings in higher-level assembly languages, and a listing of the internal controls built into the system. This form of documentation provides the new audit trail for computerized systems. File auditing software can examine the report writer's parameters for alterations, such as in the general ledger or for accounts receivable invoices.

The audit trail is used by auditors to test transactions and thereby determine whether the built-in controls are providing the checks necessary to maintain proper internal control. An effective audit trail is one which provides an auditor the opportunity to trace or reconstruct any given transaction backward or forward, from an original source of the transaction to a final total. This is also referred to as the grandfather-father-son concept of internal control.

The main intention is to assure management that the computer is processing the information—as fed into it—correctly. If incorrect data is fed in, the controls are designed to flag the transaction, or order re-transmission, or instruct the person transmitting how to transmit properly, or to log those items, which seem exceptional and report them to management. However, if fraudulent messages are transmitted in proper form and amount, the above controls will not detect them. But the same was true in manual accounting systems. Fraudulent or forged documents were no more discernible than they are now in computerized systems. Good controls discourage fraud, but can't prevent it.

Ignoring the need for auditing computerized processes is as dangerous as leaving the storeroom doors open—only the loss may be magnitudes greater. Just as the computer can process hundreds of normal transactions in a fraction of a minute, it can also generate hundreds of fraudulent transactions in the same amount of time.

## Audit Checklists

### Fraud-conducive Organizational Structure

___ The business locations of the company are widely dispersed, key documents are created at outlying locations, and evidence as to material transactions must be obtained in more than one location.

___ The company is highly diversified, having numerous different businesses, each with its own accounting system.

___ The management is dominated by one or a few individuals.

___ The company follows the practice of using different auditors for major segments.

___ The company seems to need, but lacks, an adequate internal audit staff.

___ Key financial positions, Controller, for example, do not seem to stay filled for very long.

___ The company has no outside general counsel, using special counsel for individual matters; or outside general counsel seem to be switched with some frequency.

___ The accounting and financial functions appear to be understaffed, resulting in constant crisis conditions.

___ The audit closing requires substantive adjusting entries.

### Fraud-conducive Organizational Environment

___ Lack of sufficient working capital and/or credit to continue the business.

___ The urgent desire for a continued favorable earnings record in the hope of supporting the price of the company's stock.

___ Massive demands for new capital in a developing industry and therefore developing accordingly extreme competition.

___ Dependence on a single or relatively few products, customers, or transactions for the ongoing success of the venture.

___ Little available tolerance on debt restrictions, such as maintenance of working capital, and limits on additional permissible debt, or in complying with terms of revocable licenses necessary for the continuation of the business.

___ The industry is declining or is characterized by a large number of business failures.

___ Excess capacity has befallen the company—from the energy crisis for example.

___ Existence of significant litigation—especially litigation between stockholders and management.

___ Extremely rapid expansion of business or product lines.

___ Numerous acquisitions, particularly as a diversification move.

___ In accounts receivable, difficulties in collection from a class of customers—for example, energy-related businesses and real estate investment trusts.

___ Significant inventories—the physical qualities of which require evaluation not within the expertise of the auditor.

___ A long-term manufacturing cycle for the company's products.

___ Overly optimistic earnings forecasts.

___ Significant obsolescence dangers because the company is in a high technology industry.

## Management Attitudes and Policies

### Negative

- Does not believe in checking employee references or past employment.
- Does not want to be bothered with the financial end of the business.
- Failure to enforce existing internal controls.

### Positive

- Fraud and theft exist.
- The organization could become a victim of an embezzlement.
- All potential employees should have a minimum pre-employment background check of references, work record, possible criminal record, and credit report.
- The organization needs a theft control policy and employee code of conduct.
- The policy and code should be communicated to all employees along with a fraud awareness program.
- Theft of company assets could lead to termination and prosecution.
- Not having internal controls and safeguards can lead to an embezzlement-conducive environment.
- Internal financial controls should be established, enforced, and monitored.
- A healthy skepticism that all controls are working properly.
- Internal controls and monitoring are part of management's responsibility in protecting the organization's assets.
- The organization should have an organizational chart with management responsibilities clearly defined.
- Policies and procedures should clearly describe levels of responsibilities and approvals.
- Ongoing awareness of employee morale.
- A solid awareness that failure to protect the organization's assets could result in legal liability.

## An Embezzler's Opportunity Checklist

___ What is the weakest link in this system's chain of controls?

___ What deviations from conventional good accounting practices are possible in this system?

___ How are off-line or networked transactions handled and who can authorize such transactions?

___ What would be the simplest way to compromise this system?

___ What control features in the system can be bypassed or overridden by higher authorities?

___ How can I introduce a fake debit into this system so that I can get a check issued or get my hands on cash?

___ What transaction authorization documents are easiest to access and forge?

## Red Flags of Embezzlement_____

A red flag is not actual proof but may be an indicator that something is awry. The following are a few examples:

1. Untimeliness and inaccuracy of accounting entries.
2. Too much authority vested in one person. (Inadequate separation of duties.)
3. Inadequate paper or electronic audit trails.
4. Missing records and supporting documentation.
5. Increasing reclassifications of income and expense items.
6. Increasing write-offs of receivables.
7. Increasing year-end adjusting journal entries.
8. Increasing "wash" entries, (i.e., reversed in next accounting period). (May be an indication of lapping.)
9. Build-ups of outstanding checks.
10. Build-ups of inventories, accounts receivable, and accounts payable that are inconsistent with revenue trends.
11. Missing invoices, purchase orders, receipts.
12. Customer complaints of incomplete or undelivered shipments.
13. Creditors complain about overdue invoices.
14. Second or unusual endorsements on checks.
15. Old outstanding checks.
16. Unusual patterns in deposits in transit.

## Reminder: Common Embezzlement Methods

- Forging checks and destroying them when returned with bank statements. The false transactions are concealed by forcing footings in the cash books or by raising the amounts of legitimate returned checks.

- "Accommodation" purchases not charged to employees or customers or hidden in expense accounts.
- Failing to record returned purchases, allowances, and discounts, and keeping the difference.
- Padding payrolls with rates, times, or amount produced, or adding false names, or "ghosts," to the payroll.
- Issuing checks for payment of invoices from fictitious suppliers and cashing them through the dummy.
- Pocketing the proceeds of cash sales and not recording the transactions.
- "Lapping," which is the pocketing of small amounts from incoming payments and then applying subsequent remittances on other items to cover the missing cash.
- Charging the customers more than the duplicate sales slips show and pocketing the difference.
- Misappropriating cash and charging the amounts taken to fictitious customers' accounts.
- Overloading expense accounts or advances and diverting overages to personal use.
- Carrying employees on the payroll beyond the actual severance dates.
- Withholding unclaimed wages.
- Billing stolen merchandise to fictitious accounts.
- Collusion with suppliers to overbill.
- Issuing credit for false customer claims and returns.

## Indications That Your Purchasing Staff May be "On the Take"

- Your company deals with only a handful of suppliers who don't change much. Most big jobs go to one or two firms.
- Final purchasing decisions are made by one person—with no technical staff to assess each purchase.
- The lifestyle of the purchasing executive is clearly more affluent than his salary would indicate.
- Purchasing files are not easily accessible or understandable.
- Many big orders are not covered by a single purchase order but are broken up into confusing elements, including changes and add-ons.
- There are no verified receiving reports.
- Reports from vendors are received saying that they can't get a foot in the door (20 to 25% of your vendors should change annually).
- A buyer turns down a promotion that would move him to another department.
- Purchasing staffers come in early and leave late, and never take vacations.
- Costs have risen faster than what you know is the current inflation rate.

## Manipulations Order Processing Systems

- Unique offline billing.
- Ship items with values different than invoiced.
- Ship at prices that are less than minimum for a product shipped.
- Issue credits for returned goods at prices higher than paid for or goods not returned.
- Closeout product line.
- Open items charged to and paid by the wrong customer.
- Postpone payment of an invoice (forever) by placing items in a continuous float.

## Manipulations of accounts receivable system

- Range: nickel and dime to tens of thousands of dollars.
- Misapplying checks.
- Credit adjustments.
- Wash sales.
- Customer journal adjustments.
- Truck load sales.
- Pocketing checks collected from presumably uncollectible accounts.
- Forging checks and destroying them when returned with bank statements. The false transactions are concealed by forcing footings in the cash books or by raising the amounts of legitimate returned checks.
- "Lapping," which is pocketing of small amounts from incoming payments and then applying subsequent remittances on other items to cover the missing cash.
- Misappropriating cash and charging the amounts taken to fictitious customers' accounts.

Ten commonly reported types of evidence of "management-directed" fraud in customer accounts receivable processing are:

1. Preparing customer account statements that do not indicate existing credit balances.
2. Printing statements with proper credit balance entries but failing to send them to the customers involved.
3. Issuing a special report of "suppressed" customer account credit balances for use in handling subsequent inquiries and investigations.
4. Dropping all credit balances when the customer account has been inactive for one year.
5. Printing a code on customer account statements indicating that the credit balance has been "suppressed".
6. Retaining a credit balance in the customer account record until it appears certain that the customer will not request that it be refunded, then writing it off.

7. Confusing various categories of charges and payments so as to distort the true nature of the amount owed by the customer or owed to the customer.

8. Suppressing records of mistakes that favor the customer, but always notifying the customer of mistakes that do not favor him or her.

9. "Rounding off" all odd amounts against the customer.

10. Creating "administrative transactions" that remove credit balances without the knowledge of the customer.

# Investigating Embezzlement

Investigating an embezzlement depends on how the need to investigate came about. The need may arise when one or more red flags encountered in an ongoing audit signals the existence of a possible theft scheme. In this case the scope of the examination should be expanded promptly to determine whether an embezzlement in fact has taken place, who was involved in the scheme, the amount of the actual loss, and the reasonable possibility of recovering any of the funds that have been taken.

The need for investigation may stem from complaints or allegations of dishonest activities lodged against someone. Before any other action is taken, the knowledge and trustworthiness of the sources of any such charges must be determined. This determination is best made jointly with a team that includes, at the least, a competent security investigator, the organization's legal counsel, and at least one senior executive who has experience in dealing with issues of this type. The exact makeup of this team may depend on several factors, some of them sensitive in nature. Important factors include the rank or status within the organization of the persons making the charges, the expected amount and nature of the alleged embezzlement, and the positions and power of those against whom the allegations are made.

If the company decides to go outside for help in the investigation, the first step would be to hire an attorney, then perhaps, an accountant or investigator. The attorney's duty is to establish privilege of information and to provide legal advice to the company. The accountant's letter of engagement should state that work done on the case is at the direction of the attorney and that the accountant will report findings only to the attorney. The attorney reports only legal advice to the company/client.

After the team determines the apparent validity of complaints or allegations, a separate audit should be undertaken to confirm that a loss has been sustained and to define the extent of the loss. An effort should be made to secure and corroborate a possible confession by the perpetrator. Here too, information systems auditors work as part of a joint effort to ensure that legal requirements are adhered to and that organizational goals and priorities are not ignored.

## How Embezzlement Surfaces

Evidence of employee embezzlement initially surfaces in one of several ways:

- An accounting discrepancy, irregularity, questionable transaction, or asset loss detected in the course of routine internal, external, operational, or compliance audit.
- A complaint or allegation of misconduct is made by corporate insiders, for instance, the employee's peers, subordinates, or superiors.
- A complaint or allegation of misconduct is made by corporate outsiders, for instance, suppliers, contractors, customers, competitors, police, security, or regulatory officials and friends, associates, or relatives of the employee.
- There is a notable change in the behavior of the culprit.

## Embezzlement Detection Techniques

Detection of embezzlement is possible through the conventional control concepts of separation of duties, audit trails, and periodic financial and operational audits. In addition, some combination of the following may aid detection:

1. The gathering of intelligence on the lifestyles and personal habits of employees; (This should be done in a manner that does not violate the personal privacy of these individuals and does not expose either the organization or the investigator to any form of liability.)
2. The investigation and resolution of allegations and complaints of fellow employees;
3. The logging, analysis, and settlement of any exceptions to prescribed controls and procedures;
4. The review and resolution of variances recorded in operating performance expectations (standards, goals, objectives, budgets, plans);
5. The intuition of the embezzler's superiors, and
6. Through generalized suspicion.

Each embezzler also has a pattern of theft that is somewhat unique but discernible to an experienced fraud auditor. It could be an account category that gets an inordinate amount of "padding" to cover up the loss, a particular step in the audit trail procedures that often gets bypassed, circumvented, or overridden; a fake supplier or contractor whose account balance gets manipulated; or an input document that often is fabricated, counterfeited, or forged. Most long-term embezzlement schemes, after discovery, are found to be very simple.

## The Legal Land Mines in an Internal Theft Investigation

A policy directive from management should clarify when to report an incident and to whom. A reporting policy sets up a formal system for handling possibly serious or criminal incidents as well as giving management another form of control over corporate-wide activities.

When to report? It should be done immediately upon confirmation of suspicions or when at least there is reasonable certainty that a possible criminal or damaging act has occurred. If managers wait too long to report, evidence may be lost or suspects may leave.

Upon notification, the department manager, audit or security personnel should meet with management and determine whether or not the case is open or shut or unsupported, if the evidence is sufficient, or if further investigation is necessary.

The initial interview(s) surrounding an incident, however, can be loaded with potential legal problems. The goal of this information gathering—and that is how an interview should be defined—is to get relevant facts. Jumping ahead to the incident report, it is only these relevant facts that should be in the report. Elements that are irrelevant to the cause of the incident and its effect should be left out. Always remember: every word may be reported or read at an eventual trial. As far as the question of what to do with the notes from the investigation or interview is concerned, consult with legal counsel either before conducting an investigation or shortly afterward.

Time is obviously critical in getting the facts of an incident. Keep this in mind: on average, people retain only about a third of what they see after 72 hours.

## Handling Searches and Employee Privacy

How should searches of an employee areas and equipment be conducted? Generally, an employer has to consent to a search of an employee's locker, desk, or computer and peripherals if the employer has common authority over them. Relevant factors include whether: the area/item to be searched has been set aside for the employee's exclusive or personal use (in other words, does the employee have the only key to the locker or the computer or do others have access?); the employee has been given permission to store personal information on the computer system or in the area to be searched; the employee has been advised that the desk, locker, or system may be accessed or looked at by others; there have been past inspections of the area/item and this fact is known to the employee; there is an employment policy that searches of the work area may be conducted at any time for any reason; whether the purpose of the search was business-, work-, or legal-related.

## What a Fraud Auditor Should Know about Law

What does a fraud auditor, investigator or both need to know about law? Well, at a minimum, a fraud auditor or investigator should know the following:

1. The nature and sources of substantive and procedural law, constitutional law, the common law, and criminal and civil law.

2. The distinctions between crimes that are *mala in se* (evil in and of themselves; morally wrong) and *mala prohibita* (made wrong by law or prohibited by law, but not necessarily evil or morally wrong, for instance, traffic violations).

3. The distinctions between criminal and civil law, between crimes and torts, and between federal and state crimes.

4. The elements of a crime and a tort.

5. The distinctions between criminal fraud and civil fraud.

6. The elements of criminal fraud and civil fraud.

7. The constitutional principles that apply to criminal investigations, both procedural and substantive, particularly as they relate to probable cause, search and seizure, arrest, identification, interrogation, self-incrimination, the right to counsel, due process, and equal protection.

8. The rules of evidence with respect to such things as burden of proof, presumptions, relevancy, materiality and competence, judicial notice and hearsay exceptions, that is, admissions, statements against interest, spontaneous declarations (*res gestae*), expert opinion, official records, business records, best evidence, chain of custody, and privileged communications.

9. The elements of the more common state and federal fraud statutes, (including fraud and deceit, forgery, false pretenses, tax fraud, mail fraud, securities fraud, bank fraud, procurement fraud, bankruptcy fraud, fraud by wire, benefits fraud, computer fraud, false statements, interstate theft, money laundering, Racketeer Influenced and Corrupt Organization—or RICO—and conspiracies to commit any of the above).

Where does substantive law come from? The sources of substantive law in the United States are: (1) statutes and ordinances enacted by federal, state, and local legislative bodies and regulations promulgated thereunder; (2) state and federal constitutions; and (3) the so-called common law or case law (previous opinions of state and federal supreme courts of appeal). Criminal and civil laws are accordingly derived from the above.

How does procedural law differ from substantive law? Procedural law deals with the manner in which substantive laws are passed, administered, and enforced according to due process and equal protection standards as set forth in the U.S. Constitution. For example, a criminal law passed by a legislature that has vague or ambiguous language may be ruled unconstitutional as a matter of substantive due process. Criminal laws must be clear and understandable so that people can know in advance that a particular act or inaction may be punishable as a crime. But an action or inaction alone, without criminal intent (a guilty mind), may not be punished as a crime. Intent, or *mens rea*, is a required element in most crimes (crimes that are *mala in se*). Crimes that are *mala prohibitum* usually do not require proof of criminal intent (evil motive). The mere doing of the act voluntarily, or the failure to act when required to, may be enough.

## Legal Knowledge of the Interviewer

Interviews are nonaccusatory; interrogations are accusatory. This distinction should set a framework and boundaries within an investigation. Statements made by subjects should always be voluntary if they are to stand up in court. Consider using waiver forms, signed by the subject, stating the interview was totally voluntary.

This distinction also helps make the interviewer or investigator aware of the risks and liabilities that can arise from the treatment of suspects. Brief descriptions of key legal areas are given below. Again, consult with legal counsel regarding specific investigative actions.

Defamation: wrongful disclosure of private or embarrassing facts usually requires that such information be communicated to more than one person. Any disclosure of false information could lead to a defamation suit. Defamation has two types of communication: defamation via writing, called libel; and slander, which is defamation by speech. Both are communication of false information to a third party that injures a person's reputation. Other elements of defamation have to do with the reasonable identification of the defamed person and the damage to reputation. If the defamation refers to a public figure or is a matter of public concern, it must be proved that the defamatory language was false, and that it was communicated knowingly or with a reckless disregard as to the truth or falsity of the information.

Infliction of emotional distress: may arise from the questioning of a suspect, but the conduct of the interviewer usually must be "outrageous."

False imprisonment: an unreasonable holding of a suspect for a period of time with sufficient restraint, say during questioning.

## Proving Criminal Intent

Without a voluntary and full confession, proving "criminal intent" in white-collar crime cases is the most formidable challenge to the skills and patience of investigators and auditors, mainly because evidence of such intent is usually circumstantial. You rarely have direct proof of a defendant "knowingly" or "willfully" violating larceny, embezzlement, fraud, bribery, or income tax laws. Such intent has to be inferred from other facts, such as the defendant's education, training, experience, intelligence, sophistication in the ways of business, finance, or accounting, past actions, past contradictory statements, tacit admissions, efforts to conceal records, efforts to destroy evidence, evidence of subornation or perjury or obstruction of justice, and evidence of conversion of funds to one's own use.

Defense lawyers in criminal cases often direct their whole defense to the issue of criminal intent because it is so difficult to prove. In the era of modern business, criminal intent is also very complex, so much so that reasonable doubt can be created by a clever attorney.

So how does one go about proving intent beyond a reasonable doubt? As we said, evidence of education, experience, training, intelligence, and sophistication in the ways of business, finance, and accounting may bear on the issues of generalized intent; that is, knowledge, willfulness and evil motive. But some laws have specific intent requirements. Burglary, for example, requires a breaking and entering into the residence of another in the nighttime with intent to commit a felony therein (namely, the theft of property). Larceny is the taking and carrying away of the personal property of another with the intention of permanently depriving him/her of its use.

Now let's take the example of the proverbial bookkeeper-embezzler who uses an accounts receivable lapping scheme. The bookkeeper has at least some limited right to access certain assets of his employer and the responsibility to make certain entries in the business records of the firm. In need of money for the payment of a gambling or speculation debt, high living, or family medical problems, the bookkeeper decides to "borrow" $1,000. A customer's check is received, payable to the company. The bookkeeper opens the mail, finds the check for $1,000, and substitutes it for $1,000 in the cash drawer, intending to make an entry crediting the receipt to customer A's account the next day when another $1,000 check is expected from customer B. Customer B's check is then used as the basis for covering customer A's account. The subsidiary ledger accounts of customers A and B may properly reflect their current balances because no entry debiting cash and crediting the control account for customer A's payment was made. An audit could disclose the discrepancies in accounts receivable and in the cash drawer at that point. So one further step might be taken to conceal the defalcation. If the bookkeeper can access a credit memo form and can pretend authority to issue same by forgery, customer A's account could be written off fictitiously as a discount, a rebate, allowance or even a bad debt. That effort at concealment would bear on the issue of intent or be used to rebut the bookkeeper's defense or lack of intent to embezzle.

Such evidence alone may not be enough to convict the bookkeeper of embezzlement, nor would evidence of high living, gambling, speculation, and family expense prove intent per se. Such evidence would provide a motive for embezzlement and be admissible for that purpose.

Evidence of the improper entries alone do not prove intent, either. The bookkeeper may claim in defense that the intention was not the permanent deprivation of the money to his or her employer, just the "borrowing" thereof.

Evidence of this kind of borrowing, however, implies or infers an intention to breach a fiduciary responsibility. That could help to prove criminal intent in an embezzlement case, if not in larceny. In and of themselves, these pieces of evidence may not be enough to convict. When strung together, however, they might. For example, the following facts may prove intent beyond a reasonable doubt.

1. The bookkeeper is educated, trained, and experienced in accounting.
2. The bookkeeper has a fiduciary responsibility to keep and maintain records in a timely and accurate manner.
3. The bookkeeper has been employed by the company in that capacity for five years and knows the company's accounting policies, procedures, controls, and how to make proper entries.
4. The bookkeeper's living expenses exceed his/her income by several orders of magnitude.
5. The bookkeeper was fired from two previous jobs when large amounts of money in his/her custody were found missing.

6. The lapping scheme went on for three years, and the bookkeeper kept a running tab on his/her "embezzlements." He/she now claims the running tab proves his/her intention to repay. In a bar room conversation a year ago, he/she told an acquaintance the company could be "stolen blind" by a clever thief because its controls were so weak.

7. When the cash drawer was counted during the fraud audit and investigation, there was a check from the bookkeeper to the company for a large sum of money that was used to balance the drawer. It equaled the amount of the embezzlement for the current year.

8. Evidence exists of concealment of documents, destruction of records, forged and counterfeited documents, false statements, and solicitation of false testimony.

When several of these facts are added together, a judge or jury may reasonably conclude that the defendant indeed did formulate criminal intent.

## Investigative Procedures in a Computer-Related Embezzlement

Undertaking an examination of a possible computer-related embezzlement uses methods that differ from practices that are more familiar to information systems auditors.

This type of investigation may be facilitated by the auditor:

1. Creating a separate set of work papers. This set should include hard copies of computer-generated reports, copies of operational and transaction logs, and original copies of fictitious sales invoices and similar documents. Extensive and exact records of every aspect of every activity should be maintained—for example, the date and time that someone was interviewed or the conditions under which a particular audit record was created.

2. Developing a questioning attitude and a strategy of suspicion. For example, supporting documentation should exist for all questionable disbursements, despite their source or nature. All bank account reconciliations should be reviewed to identify and resolve any unusual items or balances. In addition, the year-end journal entries should be scrutinized to locate apparently arbitrary write-offs and write-ups.

3. Maintaining a chain of custody control over these work papers. The objective is to avoid any suggestion that this documentation and any evidence associated with it has been tampered with. Extensive logs should be kept of who had access to every record, who handled it, and when it was handled.

4. Protecting this material. Routinely, all briefcases, filing cabinets, and magnetic media storage devices that are used to house any of these records should be locked. The auditor should consider employing some form of data encryption with any electronic records.

## Questions for the Investigation of Computer-Related Embezzlement

1. Are standard log-on procedures enforced? Yes___ No___
2. Does someone have administrative responsibility for access authorization? Yes___ No___
3. Are all accesses logged? Yes___ No___

   Is the user identified? Yes___ No___

   Is the date/time of access logged? Yes___ No___

   Are the functions performed identified? Yes___ No___

   Is the microcomputer or terminal identified? Yes___ No___

   Are security violations logged? Yes___ No___
4. Does the operator have restricted access to all programs and data files in the mainframe? Yes___ No___
5. Are critical or sensitive data files protected from unauthorized access? Yes___ No___
6. Are critical or sensitive data files protected from unauthorized update? Yes___ No___
7. Are there any operating or processing controls that can detect fraudulent manipulation of data? Yes___ No___

   Does software have change controllers, which limit access to critical or specified files? Yes___ No___

   Do edit programs bar mainframe data that have been changed? Yes___ No___

   Are data tagged with time and date-of-creation code? Yes___ No___

   Is simultaneous access to a file or data field barred? Yes___ No___

   Does the software provide an audit trail? Yes___ No___
8. Does the operator maintain a record of what jobs are processed? Yes___ No___
9. Are daily transactions summarized? Yes___ No___
10. Are master file balances summarized? Yes___ No___
11. Are exception reports generated? Yes___ No___
12. Is there a transaction log? Yes___ No___
13. Is the system easily modified? Yes___ No___
14. Who has access to production copies of live data or programs?

_____

_____

15. Are dial-up lines monitored and recorded for repeated failed access attempts? Yes___ No___
16. Are standard mainframe access control measures employed once dial-up connection has been made? Yes___ No___

17. Does the network or data communications system use encryption? Yes___ No___

    Does the key management program have adequate security? Yes___ No___

    Does the system have message/user identification and authentication? Yes___ No___

18. Who is responsible for authoring modifications or "patches" to accounting or bookkeeping software programs _____

19. How are wire funds transfers initiated and payment orders authorized? ___

20. Who is allowed to send a funds transfer? What are the identification and verification methods for the sender and the payment order? _____

21. Do wire transfer security measures include:

    Imposing limits on the amount of any transfer? Yes___ No___

    Transfers payable only from an authorized account? Yes___ No___

    Prohibiting any transfer that exceeds specific credit limits or account balances? Yes___ No___

    Limiting transfer to authorized beneficiaries? Yes___ No___

## Electronic Evidence

With computers often the main tool used to create results used in financial statements, auditors must look at computer safeguards and controls and the problems of authentication of computer-generated evidence. The differences in evidence have implications for devising levels of computer security and data storage and archiving as well as investigating possible financial statement irregularities.

There are essentially four types of electronic or computer generated evidence: data, illustrations, simulations, and electronically-imaged documents.

Electronic evidence can be created, altered, stored, copied, and moved easily and quickly. Electronic evidence will always need to be authenticated in some way; one must be ready to show that the process of production for a specific computer system is reliable. Authentication may be established by "evidence describing a process or system used to produce a result and showing that the process or system produces an accurate result." (*Federal Rules of Evidence*, 901(b)(9))

For example, the general legal foundation for admission of computer evidence/business records should give proof of:

- The manner in which the basic data were initially entered into the system;
- The entrance of the data in the regular course of business;
- The reliability of the computer equipment used to produce and store records and, if called for, to produce a hard copy;

- The time during which data were entered was within a reasonable period after the events recorded by the person having personal knowledge of the events;
- Adequate measures were taken to ensure accuracy of the entered data;
- Effective data storage and security measures;
- The reliability of the programs used to process the data;
- The measures taken to verify the accuracy of the computer programs;
- The time and method of creating the hard copy.

To be competent, evidence, regardless of its form, must be both valid and relevant. Accessing and evaluating information processed and stored on a computer poses problems in determining the competence of the evidence.

## An Outline of Criminal Investigation and Its Legal Implications ____

1. A putative criminal act is reported, discovered or discerned.

   Is the act in fact a violation of a criminal law? Yes__ No___

   If so, what specific law or laws?

   _____

   _____

   When was the act committed? (statute of limtations)_____

   _____

   Where was the act committed? (jurisdiction, venue)_____

   How was the act committed? (modus operandi)_____

   _____

   Who committed the act? (legal capacity)_____

   How can the actor be identified and located? (arrest, search and seizure)

   _____

   Why was the act committed? (motive, intent)_____

   _____

2. What evidence links the criminal act to the suspect?

   _____

   Are witnesses to the criminal act available? Yes___ No___

   Are these witnesses legally competent, credible, and willing to testify? Yes___ No___

   Can they positively identify the suspect? Yes___ No___

   Are documents to prove the charge available? Yes___ No___

   In whose legal custody are these documents?_____

   Will these documents be surrendered voluntarily or will judicial processes be required? (subpoena) Yes___ No___

   Do the documents speak for themselves or will they require a foundation for their introduction? (public vs. private records) Yes___ No___

   Comment: _____

Are the documents kept in the regular course of trade or business?
Yes___ No___

Are tools, means, instruments, and fruits of the crime available?
Yes___ No___

How were these acquired? (Incident leading up to arrest, execution of search warrant, voluntarily submitted?

Found at the crime scene? Discovered by accident?_____

---

Have these items been marked, identified, and kept in a secured place?
Yes___ No___

Has their transfer been recorded as to date, person, and purpose? (Chain of custody) Yes___ No___

3. Has the suspect been arrested? Yes___ No___ With or without a warrant?_____

4. Was the suspect advised of his or her rights? Yes___ No___

5. Was the suspect searched? Yes___ No___

6. Was any incriminating evidence found on his or her person or in the immediate area of arrest? Yes___ No___

7. Was the suspect interrogated? Yes___ No___ Was it before or after having been advised of his or her rights?_____

8. Did the suspect make any spontaneous admissions of guilt? Yes___ No___

9. Did the suspect make a confession? Yes___ No___

   Voluntarily? Yes___ No___

   Were any oral promises made of leniency? Yes___ No___

   Were any oral promises made of intercessions with prosecutorial or judicial authorities? Yes___ No___

   Were any other assurances made? Yes___ No___

During an investigation, evidence is gathered of the material elements of the crime (*corpus delicti*). That information is then referred to a prosecuting authority who reviews the facts and available evidence and decides whether they are suitable and adequate to justify a conviction. If so, a formal accusation is made in the form of an indictment or information—usually an indictment for a felony charge and an information for a misdemeanor in federal cases. But private citizens may also initiate a formal accusation by filing a complaint with an officer of the court, or in some jurisdictions, an officer of the law.

## Investigating Embezzlement: An Outline and Checklist of Legal Issues

An investigation into a possible embezzlement, larceny, or fraud seeks to determine: if a criminal act has occurred; identification of the suspect/perpetrators; an accurate loss estimate; if there is enough evidence for prosecution by law enforcement; or if the evidence gathered warrants only recovery via restitution or under an insurance policy. The investigation also provides information for legal advice given to the corporation and is, therefore, part of the defense of the corporation against possible compliance-related liability.

The following outline and checklist highlight the more significant steps to take and questions to examine in developing a planned, efficient response to an embezzlement, the recovery of assets, and the minimization of compliance litigation risk.

I. Types of misconduct or illegal acts that would or should trigger an investigation
    A. Possible criminal misconduct by senior officers, managers, employees, or agents
    B. Misconduct that produces possible liability for the corporation

II. When to initiate an internal investigation
    A. When the corporation becomes aware that its officers, executives, managers, or employees have or are involved in acts of embezzlement or larceny against the organization, which if not resolved could lead to loss of assets or harm the organization's reputation
    B. When the implications are fully understood; that is, if the perpetrator is known, whether the embezzlement was carried out by one or more employees, if the legal risk exposures have been identified, and if possible damages have been estimated.

III. Elements of the investigation plan
    A. What is the nature and source of possible personnel misconduct?
        1. Rumor, accusation, gossip; list any credible sources
        2. Company fraud or ethics hotline, audits, compliance reviews, vendor complaints
        3. Law enforcement contact
    B. Type of misconduct
        1. Criminal
        2. Civil
        3. Regulatory
    C. Who is involved and is the misconduct systemic?
        1. Single, rogue employee
        2. Employees and lower-level management
        3. Mid-level management
        4. Senior officers
    D. What is the level of seriousness and corporate exposure to the attendant risks?
        1. Criminal liability
        2. Substantial monetary damages
        3. Injury to reputation
        4. Other significant harm
    E. Who should direct the internal investigation?
        1. In-house counsel

2. Outside counsel

3. Other

F. What resources should be used to conduct an efficient internal investigation?

    1. In-house auditors and investigators

    2. Auditors, investigators, and technicians hired and controlled by outside counsel

    3. Combination of in-house and outside auditors and investigators

G. Adopt board of directors resolution for directing the investigation

## Internal Corporate Investigation: Directing the Investigation _____

The following outline suggests critical initial steps in an internal corporate investigation. This outline starts from the premise that an internal investigation is necessary, and that a decision has been made to learn the extent and seriousness of a specific corporate problem—a problem that may or may not, at some point, lead to the notification and involvement of government or criminal justice agencies. The objectives of this outline are to provide guidance on conducting a prompt, efficient, and diligent investigation, one that offers maximum legal protection to the corporate entity.

1. The Board of Directors of the corporation meets and appoints a special committee to:

- Direct the investigation;

- Retain outside counsel.

An enabling resolution by the Board should say that the special committee will direct a legal study and investigation and that it should retain outside legal counsel to provide the corporation, through the special committee, legal advice based on its findings.

2. Outside legal counsel is authorized to conduct the investigation and is:

- Given autonomy to conduct a professional investigation and inquiry;

- Authorized to procure such assistance as necessary, such as independent accountants and investigators;

- Authorized to interview any employees of the corporation who might have knowledge of the facts;

- Authorized to analyze any and all information gathered from sources and materials inside and outside the corporation.

3. Outside counsel should meet on a regular basis with the special committee:

- Minutes or some record of the meetings should be made. Obvious sensitive topics need not be recorded. Some evidence of these meetings is needed, however, to establish the diligence of the special committee and counsel.

4. Guidelines for conducting the internal investigation:

- It is the responsibility of the investigators to report only to the special committee; there is no responsibility to report to corporate management;

- Legal counsel at all times must make decisions on assistance and investigative materials based on the establishment of attorney-client privilege and work product rule;
- If company personnel are used in the investigation, they must be instructed that during the investigation their work product and findings are to be given only to the outside legal counsel;
- Independent accountants, auditors, investigators, and others should be engaged to assist and report exclusively to the outside legal counsel. Again, such engagements should be set up so as not to jeopardize the attorney-client privilege or work product rule. Services of independent experts should be procured through outside counsel and the work done under its direction.

  Results of the work should become the exclusive property of the outside law firm; all communications are to be conducted exclusively with outside counsel, and all professional services paid for by the outside counsel. All of the above should be included in a retainer letter or contract between the law firm and the independent service supplier.

5. At the conclusion of the investigation, outside counsel advises the special committee on its findings and suggested legal action.
6. The special committee reports to the corporation's board of directors on the investigation and the advice given by outside legal counsel.
7. The board of directors decides on what action, if any, to take.
8. Information control and access strategies: In internal corporate investigations of possible criminal misconduct, the defense and prosecution have distinct strategies related to information. For the defense of the corporation, the strategy must be to control access to critical information. (Review the primary legal methods of controlling access with legal counsel: the attorney-client privilege, the self-evaluation privilege, and the work product rule.)
9. Information gathering and evaluation, Phase 1:
- Document reviews and identification; separate privileged documents; produce an index of documents;
- Initial audit review;
- Identify prospective interviewees: employees/agents possibly having knowledge of location of or removal of documents; parties involved in possible wrongdoing;
- Write and distribute letter of instruction from senior executive officer or legal counsel to each employee to be interviewed; advise that the attorney represents the corporation and that employee may retain personal attorney;
- Conduct survey (via interviews or form) with selected personnel;
- For all interviews, use two interviewers, counsel and legal assistant; do not produce verbatim transcripts and quotes or factual descriptions of the substance of interviews; instead create only summary memos and notes that contain "counsel's mental impressions" throughout.
10. Corporate prosecution and termination policy: Determine the corporation's policy toward prosecuting employee embezzlement. Is there a written policy to this effect? Has the corporation a past record of prosecution?

11. Possible criminal violation: It is often difficult at the outset of an investigation to establish whether or not there has been a specific federal or state criminal violation of a specific statute, or what jurisdiction has venue. Look for the following elements before deciding on the exact nature of the possible offense or misconduct:

- Are there indications of intent to commit a wrongful act?
- Disguise of purpose (falsities, misrepresentations)?
- Reliance by the suspect on ignorance or carelessness of victim?
- Voluntary victim action to assist the suspect?
- Concealment of the violation?
- Dollar amount of the larceny or embezzlement?

12. Liability risk assessment: If the violation is known, review the statute(s), assess the position of the organization regarding culpability, defenses, possible damages, cooperation with the prosecutor, voluntary disclosure, or internal resolution.

- It should be determined if a civil lawsuit and its less demanding burden of proof is a better legal strategy.
- If recovery of loss is primary, are insurance/bonding policies sufficient?

13. Case theory and evidence: Most investigations have a theory of the case at the outset. This usually means there has been a review of the applicability of particular criminal statutes to the initially known facts of the case. During information/evidence gathering, the theory of the case may be modified or develop in a different direction. This is simply a determination, based on new information, of which violations are most clearly demonstrated by the evidence gathered and what additional evidence maybe required, as well as what evidence might be needed to negate defenses.

14. Information sources: Information comes from either persons or things. In internal corporate investigations, things are usually business records and recorded information about specific activities of personnel and executives. Information can also come from persons inside and outside the business. To gather information most efficiently and thoroughly, it is vital for the investigator to know the system of the organization—its paper flow, disposition of documents, its procedures for claims, payments, and so forth. Also important is knowledge of personnel and job functions—who is most likely to have what information.

15. Information and evidence gathering: During the course of any investigation a lot of information is gathered. Only a small portion of the total will wind up as evidence. Evidence, then, is actually distilled information. The distillation process is one of gathering, examination, and appraisal plus a constant testing against both the theory of the case and possible violations of law.

- Determine if the organization has done previous compliance reviews, audits, or investigations that could be useful to the current investigation.
- If so, determine the results to date and obtain and secure all reports and evidence gathered.
- Determine who should be interviewed.

- Determine which reports and documents should be examined.

16. Review with legal counsel laws affecting internal investigations.
    - Discovery privileges.
    - Document retention and destruction.
    - Employee-related law, such as privacy, defamation, false imprisonment, harassment, witness tampering, and obstruction of justice.
    - Searches and seizures.

17. Expert witness/technical assistance: Contact expert witnesses that may be needed for the investigation, such as information systems technicians, accountants/auditors, or specialists in specific areas of compliance.

18. Security and storage of evidence:
    - Mark documents, reports, surveys, interviews, and other materials relevant to the case, according to its assigned level of proprietary information security.
    - Secure the documentation for possible litigation and, if necessary, lock up materials such as magnetic media or printouts in appropriate storage, such as fire-resistant safes or those designed for storing media.

19. Case report by chief investigator: Utilizing the evidence and testimony gathered, report the findings to legal counsel for disposition.

20. Counsel's report of findings of fact and legal opinion: Report may be given verbally or written to the board of directors, the audit committee, the CEO or other responsible corporate officers. It should cover:
    - Case chronology;
    - Type of misconduct and degree of seriousness;
    - Individual employee(s) involved; profile possible indictable suspects(s);
    - If misconduct is systemic (give level of management and location within corporation);
    - Extent of possible corporate liability; does misconduct affect materiality issues, accuracy of tax filings, fiduciary responsibilities; cite specific statute(s) for possible litigation by the government;
    - Disclosure requirements; if optional disclosure, what are the legal benefits and risks;
    - Status of evidence and witnesses;
    - Internal control weaknesses and corrective actions that should be taken;
    - The summary: give an opinion on what action to take and when regarding insurance recovery, civil lawsuit, or criminal prosecution of perpetrators.

# Reporting Embezzlement

This embezzlement reporting form (seen in Appendix 2) presents a suggested format for a final report to use in documenting actions surrounding an embezzlement. As with any investigative reporting form, you should consult with legal counsel before using it within your organization.

The report form has been designed to fulfill three purposes:

1. To provide a format for recording the essential details of an embezzlement.
2. To afford the preparer with a framework for analyzing the embezzlement case.
3. To develop improved management policies, controls, and audits to detect and prevent embezzlement.

The form covers various elements of an embezzlement. In reporting an embezzlement, it is imperative to be precise. The investigation, as well as the reporting, must proceed as if the outcome will be adjudicated. Recording exact times, dates, names of persons, and specific descriptions of evidence are critical in a civil or criminal investigation or litigation. In short, stick to facts, discount hearsay, rumor, or opinion, and record only what is relevant to the cause of the incident and its effect. Always keep in mind that your every word may be repeated or read at an eventual trial.

## Interim Reports

The first interim report should describe the case review and determine whether the incident deserves further investigation. Subsequent reports should give the status of the investigation, including the suspects, authorities contacted, evidence gathered, and possible outcome, be it legal, civil, restitution, or otherwise.

## The Final Report

The report form found in Appendix 2 has questions for documenting an embezzle-ment. All the information to fill out may not be essential in every case. The following paragraphs provide more detail on the questions in this form.

Personal information: Give a precise and appropriate description of the perpetrator and that person's job function, duties, and experience. The same applies to suspects or accomplices, if any, and their relationship to the perpetrator and the company.

Dates and time: Because an incident may take place over several months or years, the time or duration of the incident is very important. Again, be precise; however, if exact dates are not known, give approximate time frame.

Description of the incident: Be specific about the incident; in other words, was it a larceny, embezzlement, willful misapplication, defalcation, forgery, larceny, concealment, misappropriation, malfeasance, or some other kind of fraud or theft? The nature of the incident and which laws were violated may be difficult to identify at first, but by the final report, legal counsel should have it defined. The possibility that several laws may have been broken, or that there may be an applicable law that is not apparent at the outset, should always be considered.

Where the embezzlement occurred: A description of where the incident occurred should give the division, department and operation plus the specific processes or transaction area, such as purchasing, receiving, accounts payable, payroll, receivables, and so forth.

If the incident involved data processing, be specific in your descriptions of the data processing operation, computer system, application programs or files involved. Remember, in court you may have to show how the system operated normally in order to prove that a manipulation occurred.

How the embezzlement was perpetrated: Here you must describe exactly where, within the operation or a particular system, the incident occurred and how the manipulation, collusion, or abuse was accomplished.

Proof of loss information and estimates: Estimating, with some precision, the dollar value loss for restitution or fidelity insurance claims can be critical in possible future recovery action in a civil suit. Consult with the risk/insurance manager on what is excluded from damages coverage.

Incident discovery: How the incident was discovered can have important consequences for both the investigation and prosecution. If the incident was discovered during an audit, you can use the documentation generated by the audit and have the auditor as a technical advisor or expert witness. If you were tipped by an informer, you have to consider reliability and motives.

Incident investigation: Give a concise and accurate description of the investigative process, as well as the personnel and authorities contacted, for example, security, internal auditor, legal counsel, or law enforcement.

Evidence: Describe all evidence that demonstrated the perpetrator's intention to commit a specific criminal act; indicate the collector and custodian of specific evidence and where it is preserved.

Interviews: Include the name of the interviewer, who was interviewed and the time and date; also summarize key points of the interview and give the names of witnesses present.

Case disposition: The final actions taken by the organization may be legal, civil, insurance/bonding recovery or restitution. Final comments on case disposition should indicate the current employment status of the perpetrator, whether suspended, resigned, terminated, or whereabouts unknown. Also discuss what, if any, restitution arrangements have been made.

Security and controls: Describe the security or control systems or procedures that were compromised in carrying out the embezzlement. If the cause was weak controls, poor monitoring, lax security, less-than-thorough audits, or indifferent management, give an objective appraisal of the problem and personnel involved.

Corrective actions: Answer these questions: How could this embezzlement have been prevented? What specific security and audit policies, procedures, personnel, or equipment should be improved or added to guard against future occurrences?

# *Learning to Think Like a Thief: Developing Fraud Scenarios*

An effective fraud auditor must learn to think like an on-the-job thief. Such thieves are constantly testing system weaknesses for easy entry points. Fraud auditors, too, must study control mechanisms to find areas of weakness as a test of the adequacy of internal controls, but also to theorize about the specific vulnerabilities that may exist given those weaknesses.

Pinpointing weak links in the chain of command (poor managers) and chain of controls (poor management) is what fraud auditing is generally about. Identifying weak links and theorizing about their consequences is what developing fraud scenarios is about. Let your imagination run wild on the eight cases that follow:

1. Blank sales credit memo forms are on an open shelf in the sales department. The memos are not pre-serially numbered but are manually assigned a sequential number by a sales clerk who uses a typewriter to imprint the number on the form. Authorizations for the issuance of such memos are routed to her by the assistant sales manager without counter-signature. The authorization form is also not pre-serially numbered. The clerk attaches the authorization request to the company's file copy in the sales department, then mails a copy to the customer and sends a copy to the accounts receivable section, which then enters the credit to the customer's account on an online terminal. The sales department clerk and the receivables section clerk who enters the credit memo are friends and often visit one another's home.

1. What are the opportunities for fraud and whom would they involve?

_____

_____

_____

_____

_____

2. The purchasing department's manual specifies that purchase orders are to be pre-serially numbered, issued only on a requisition by an authorized department head and cosigned by the director of purchasing and the specific purchasing agent who is assigned the products or services called for in the request. Vendors of products are to be approved by the department head and director of purchasing. Such approvals are to be based on the quality of past materials purchased, pricing, timely past deliveries, and financial reliability.

An annual review of all vendors who sell more than $500,000 of goods, materials, and services is also required for the purpose of updating the approved vendor file. The quality control department head and the director of purchasing are assigned that responsibility.

In the course of your review of internal controls, you found (1) a supply of blank purchase orders without pre-serialized numbers, (2) purchasing agents that have never been rotated, (3) a year-long supply contract for heating oil that was not subject to competitive bids, (4) that the largest single vendor of critical materials for production is in receivership, (5) that the vendors have not been evaluated for three years.

What are the opportunities for fraud and whom would they involve?

_____

_____

_____

_____

_____

3. A customer is in your bank today and says he has a problem. (He was called by your assistant branch manager yesterday, while you were out playing golf, and told his account was overdrawn.)

The customer is a retailer and says an overdraft in his account is impossible because he never has less than a $10,000 balance. The account is never drawn down below that figure. His bookkeeper regularly advises him when the balance is getting close to that level, and he immediately makes a deposit.

You go to your branch terminal and ask the computer to display his account's activity for the current month. Sure enough, until three days ago, there had always been a minimum balance of at least $10,000. There is no indication that any of the checks he recently deposited were drawn on accounts with non-sufficient funds. Three days ago, however, the retailer claims he deposited a $15,000 check from an account at another bank into his main account. That deposit, however, does not show up on your screen. You ask him whom the check was made payable to, and he states it was made payable to "cash." To add further to the mystery, there is indeed a $15,000 deposit (which took care of the overdraft), but it is recorded on the statement as having been made yesterday.

What do you do?

_____

_____

_____

_____

_____

4. You are employed as an undercover operative at a men's clothing store in a large shopping center. Ostensibly, your job is selling shirts. On your first day of employment, you notice the cash register clerk remove cash from the register and a place a piece of paper therein. The register is a point-of-sale (POS) terminal. The POS used at the store satisfies a number of purposes. It records sales, updates inventory, re-orders stock when supplies are low, checks customer credit status and approves customers for credit card sales. The POS is also used to record customer returns and issue credits. And in the event of error, the clerk can void sales.

How can such a system be compromised? What was the cash register clerk up to?

_____

_____

_____

_____

_____

5. You are working undercover at a distribution center of a company that makes consumer electronic products such as VCRs, microwave ovens, tape players and TV sets. We will call it Consumer Electronic Products Inc. (CEPI). CEPI is an American company with manufacturing facilities in the U.S. Its profits have been sagging of late due to foreign competition. Its stock market performance reflects its poor fortunes in the marketplace. The company has had three presidents in the last five years. Prior to that, the company had been in the stable hands of its founder, who ran the company with an iron fist for the previous 30 years.

The company has eight manufacturing facilities and four major distribution centers in the U.S. The largest distribution center is in New Jersey, where you work, followed by Chicago, Los Angeles, and Atlanta. Inventory shrinkage is a problem at each of the centers, but New Jersey leads the pack. Last year, it had a shrinkage factor of 8 percent on an average daily inventory of $20 million ($1.6 million).

The company was very concerned about the loss, so it engaged the services of your agency. The agency now has three undercover operatives employed at the facility. Thus far, you have uncovered a ring of marijuana smokers among the warehouse workers and two users of cocaine on the shipping/receiving dock. Another operative works in the office as a clerk and reports the clerical staff is dispirited about a new order entry system that continues to have a high rate of down time.

The office clerk has also discovered that a lot of inventory errors seem to be made. Some items are double counted; others aren't counted at all. Inventory is often missing, so back orders are common. Billing errors occur frequently too. So a number of correcting journal entries have to be made to correct software errors, hardware errors, mathematical errors, errors in routing orders, customer misinformation, and so forth. In addition, there is much transferring of goods between the various distribution centers. These intracompany transfers seem to have higher error rates than those involving customers.

What could a clever thief get away with in such an environment?

_____

_____

_____

_____

6. A fruitful area for an embezzler is the manipulation of shipments, sales, and billing procedures. The objective here is to confuse the company into:

- Shipping a product to a customer without sending an invoice.
- Shipping one thing and billing the customer for something else.
- Billing a shipment at the wrong price.
- Granting improper credits or adjustments on returned or damaged products.
- Manipulating the sales commissions, allowances, and discounts on merchandise shipped.

How would you go about committing each act?

_____

_____

_____

_____

7. Building an inventory fraud scenario: The facts: ABC Company is a manufacturer of electronic components, including integrated circuits, designed for use in large system computer mainframes. Its business is international and has been highly profitable in the past. Current competition in the industry is keen, and profits have been falling of late. Discrepancies were found in its most recent audit pertaining to its supplies of integrated circuits ($200,000 at manufacturer's cost) and its supplies of gold and platinum ($150,000 at cost).

Its inventory accounting system seems adequate for its size and complexity of operations. Physical security over raw materials and finished goods consists of caged rooms that are inaccessible except through locked doors, which limit access to certain authorized employees with magnetic cards. Withdrawal orders from these stocks must be in writing on a pre-serialized stock-withdrawal form and approved by any one of the three shift production superintendents.

A quantity of gold was withdrawn on July 27, 1981, worth $27,500. The withdrawal order contained the forged signature of the night production superintendent. Any one of five night foremen delivered the forged withdrawal to the store's department night manager. He has no recollection regarding who may have presented the withdrawal to him, but production scheduling records show that only three of the night foremen were supervising component assemblies requiring stocks of gold.

Store clerks are searched by metal detectors when they leave the storeroom. On July 26, 1981, the only entries logged are those of the store's clerks.

Each night foreman working on the evening of July 27, 1981, has been with the firm for at least 10 years. Each is trusted and highly regarded by management. The clerk on duty that night is also a veteran employee, and his performance has been excellent. But his brother-in-law, an assembler in the plant on the day shift, was fired for insubordination two months before the alleged theft took place.

Suspects: Thus far, the suspects include the night shift foremen and the store's clerk. But there is no guarantee that the theft was committed on the night shift. It may have been perpetrated at any time on July 27, 1981, because the stock requisitions are only date-stamped, not date- and time-stamped. Therefore, day and afternoon foremen and store clerks cannot be ruled out.

Motivations: The night shift store clerk seems to be a prime suspect at the moment. His brother-in-law's termination may have caused him to lash out at the company. But to have accomplished the theft himself, he would have had to (1) gain access to store's blank requisition forms, fabricate the withdrawal data, and forge the night superintendent's signature; and (2) bypass the metal detector to get the gold out of the cage.

Means and Methods: If that is the case, it is possible that the theft was accomplished by collusion with one of the night foremen (who do not pass through the detector and who have access to blank stores requisitions), or with the plant guard who operates the detection equipment, or with both the foreman and guard as coconspirators.

Develop a theory of the case:

_____

_____

_____

_____

_____

8. The Grandma Mason case: You are the branch manager of a thriving bank and you take great pride in your branch's growth record and the high caliber of your personnel. One day an elderly customer, Grandma Mason, age 82, comes in and says that she wants to renew her one-year, $10,000 certificate of deposit. She says she was not advised that it had come up for renewal but recalled that it was exactly one year ago that she purchased it. She also recalled that it was a very busy day at the

bank and that the teller had told her the certificate would be mailed to her when her check for the $10,000 cleared. However, she never received the certificate. Her personal check did clear so she assumed everything was all right. Besides, it was January, and she hated to go out into the cold.

You make a quick search of the certificate of deposit files on your branch's terminal, but there is no such account in Grandma Mason's name. You ask Grandma who the teller was. She cannot recall specifically. She thinks the teller was a middle-aged woman. There are several tellers who match that description. Grandma looks them over and says none of them look familiar. Your branch personnel turnover rate is the best in the bank but it still runs around 25 percent per year. Furthermore, because of the bank's volume and good management, your branch is used for training, and three or four tellers a month who come through the branch to be trained are later assigned to other branches.

A year ago, there were eight regular tellers and four trainees employed on the day Grandma said she bought the certificate of deposit. Two of the tellers worked the drive-in window, with one trainee under their supervision. The other nine (six regulars, three trainees) worked the lobby windows. Two of the nine regular tellers have since left the bank, but the trainees are still with the bank, working at different branches.

What preliminary steps would you take?

Would you verify the fraud first or begin to search for suspects?

How might you go about verifying the fraud?

What documents would you secure? Who would you interview? When would you call the bank's internal auditor? The FBI?

Would you take handwriting samples from all the tellers who were there a year ago?

_____

_____

_____

_____

_____

# Leader's Guide to Fraud Awareness Training

This leader's guide proposes methods of using and customizing the enclosed instructional materials. The training materials provide a flexible, cost-effective program, easily administered, with provisions for modifying and updating the information as necessary. A rough script suggests areas where company-specific information could be inserted, or where more detailed information on a specific subject can be found in the book.

The fraud awareness program's training leader is urged to customize the materials to make them as relevant to his or her organization as possible. The leader/instructor is also urged to set company-specific learning objectives for the program. The instructor should specify the knowledge he or she wants the attendee to have as a result of having taken the fraud awareness training program. In devising learning objectives, the question for the instructor is: what do I want the attendee to know when he or she finishes the program?

Suggested learning objectives for the program could be to:

- Recognize the various types of fraud, larceny, and embezzlement and how they occur
- Understand the legal definitions of theft, fraud, larceny, and embezzlement
- Understand the organization's ethics policy and code of conduct regarding theft and embezzlement
- Know company policy and procedures on reporting possible wrongdoing by employees
- Have an awareness of the importance of internal controls for both the employee and the organization

An informal environment is best for this training, with small groups preferable to encourage a discussion of individual views.

An evaluation form is included to document participant attendance as well as to express an opinion on the training. Additionally, the form will provide documentation and evidence that the organization made a concerted effort to communicate to employees its policies and codes of conduct regarding embezzlement, theft, and fraud.

## Fraud Awareness Training Materials

The artwork and title graphics in the program are designed and sized to be made into overhead transparencies. This can be done on either a plain paper copier or on a transparency maker.

Overhead transparencies and still projection techniques are easily adaptable to small or large groups. Information can be presented in systematic, developmental sequences. And, the instructor/leader has complete control of the presentation.

While the presentation is designed as a stand-alone program, space is left on some overheads so you can add company-specific information; or, the presentation can easily be modified by deleting visuals or by the addition of your own overheads that are, again, relevant to your organization.

# Training Participant Feedback Form

Date_____ Time_____ Instructor_____

Participant_____ Dept._____

1. Did the instructor discuss the learning objectives of the training? Yes____ No___

2. Did you understand the learning objectives? Yes____ No____

3. What is one idea, concept, thing, or technique that you plan to immediately apply on your job?_____

_____

4. I learned that I _____

_____

_____

5. I discovered that I _____

_____

_____

6. I resolved to _____

_____

_____

7. Did the training materials fit the learning objectives? Yes____ No____

8. Were the training materials difficult to read and understand? Yes____ No____

9. Please give your suggested improvements to the training materials and any other additional comments: _____

_____

_____

_____

_____

_____

_____

_____

_____

Your signature_____

Date_____Time_____

# Embezzlement Reporting Form

Title:_____Report number:_____

Company:_____Division:_____

Prepared by:_____Date:_____


## Personal Information_____

Name:_____Title:_____

Department:_____Salary:_____Age:_____Sex:__

Years/months with company:_____Marital status:_____

Home address:_____

City:_____State:__Zip:_____Phone:_____

Background/position:_____

Description of suspect(s)/accomplice(s), if any:_____

_____

Relationship to perpetrator and company:_____

_____

## Specifics of Incident _____

Date and duration of incident: Start date:_____

End date:_____

Nature of incident:_____

_____

_____

Incident location (give department and operation involved):_____

_____

_____

If data processing system involved, what specific equipment, application programs, or operating systems were manipulated or abused?_____

_____

_____

_____

How was the embezzlement perpetrated?_____

_____

_____

_____

_____

## Loss Information _____

Direct loss (estimation or precise dollar value):_____

_____

_____

Describe equipment or other items lost and give total and individual dollar values:_____

_____

_____

## Description of Investigation _____

How was the incident discovered (audit, informer, accidental discovery)?_____

_____

_____

How was the incident investigated?_____

_____

_____

_____

_____

Describe the evidence gathered:_____

_____

_____

_____

Describe the perpetrator and/or suspect(s) interview:_____

_____

_____

_____

Is a copy of employee/perpetrator statement attached? Yes ___No___

## Disposition of the Case

If legal action was taken, supply the following information:

1. Case citation:_____

2. Location (court, city, county, state):_____

3. Documents prepared in case:_____

_____

_____

_____

_____

Comments on the above:_____

_____

_____

Disposition of the incident (other than legal; for instance, no charge filed, restitution accepted, employee(s) dismissed):_____

_____

_____

Identify and give dollar values for items recovered:_____

_____

_____

Comments on security, control, audit or management weakness relevant to this case:_____

_____

_____

_____

Recommended corrective actions to prevent further incidents:_____

_____

_____

_____

Case history reviewed by:_____Date:_____

Signature:_____

# Bibliography

Akin, Richard H. *The Private Investigator's Basic Manual.* Springfield, Ill.: Charles C. Thomas, 1976.

Albrecht, W. *Fraud: Bringing Light to the Dark Side of Business.* Burr Ridge, Ill.: Irving Professional Publishing, 1995.

Androphy, J. *White Collar Crime.* Colorado Springs: Shepard's/McGraw-Hill, 1992.

Arkin, Stanley et al. *Business Crime: Criminal Liability of the Business Community.* New York: Matthew Bender, 1981.

Audit Commission, *A Study of Internal Frauds in Banks.* Chicago: Bank Administration Institute, 1972.

Bailey, F. Lee, and Henry B. Rothblatt. *Investigation and Preparation of Criminal Cases.* Rochester: Lawyers Co-operative, 1970.

Bender, David. *Computer Law: Evidence and Procedure.* New York: Matthew Bender, 1978.

Bintliff, Russell. *White Collar Crime: Prevention and Detection.* Englewood Cliffs, N.J.: Prentice Hall, 1993.

Block, Dennis J., and Marvin J. Pickholz. *The Internal Corporate Investigation.* New York: Practicing Law Institute, 1980.

Blum, Richard H. *Deceivers and Deceived.* Springfield, Ill.: Charles C. Thomas, 1972.

Bologna, Jack. *Computer Crime: Wave of the Future.* Madison, Wis.: Assets Protection, 1981

Bologna, Jack. *Handbook on Corporate Fraud.* Stoneham, Mass.: Butterworth-Heinemann 1993.

Bologna, G. Jack, and Robert J. Lindquist. *Fraud Auditing and Forensic Accounting: New Tools and Techniques.* New York: John Wiley & Sons, 1987.

Bologna, Jack and Paul Shaw. *Fraud Awareness Manual.* Madison, Wis.: Assets Protection, 1992.

Brickey, Kathleen. *Corporate Criminal Liability.* Deerfield, Ill: Callaghan & Co., 1989.

Brown, L. *The Legal Audit: Corporate Internal Investigation.* New York: Clark Boardman, 1990.

Cadmus, Bradford. *Internal Control Against Fraud and Waste.* New York: Prentice Hall, 1953.

Coleman, James William. *The Criminal Elite: The Sociology of White Collar Crime.* New York: St. Martin's Press, 1985.

Comer, Michael. *Corporate Fraud.* New York: McGraw-Hill, 1977.

Committee of Sponsoring Organizations of the Treadway Commission (COSO). *Internal Control—Integrated Framework.* New York: The Committee of Sponsoring Organizations of the Treadway Commission, 1992.

Cressey, Donald R. *Other People's Money: The Social Psychology of Embezzlement.* New York: Free Press, 1953.

Elliott, Robert K., and John J. Willingham. *Management Fraud: Detection and Deterrence.* New York: Petrocelli Books, 1980.

Federal Bureau of Investigation. *Introduction to Books and Records.* Quantico, Va: FBI Academy, 1975.

Forensic Services Directory. Princeton, N.J.: National Forensic Center (annual).

Frank, P., ed. *Litigation Services Handbook.* New York: John Wiley & Sons, 1990.

Geis, Gilbert. *On White Collar Crime.* Lexington, Mass.: Lexington Books, 1982.

Glekel, Jeffrey, ed. *Business Crimes: A Guide for Corporate and Defense Counsel.* New York: Practicing Law Institute, 1982.

Glick, Rush G., and Robert S. Newson. *Fraud Investigation.* Springfield, Ill.: Charles C. Thomas, 1974.

Goldblatt, M. *Preventive Law in Corporate Practice.* New York: Matthew Bender, 1991.

Grau, J.J., and B. Jacobson. *Criminal and Civil Investigation Handbook.* New York: McGraw-Hill, 1981.

Green, Gary S. *Occupational Crime.* Chicago: Nelson-Hall, 1990.

Gup, B. *Bank Fraud.* Chicago: Bank Administration Institute, 1991.

Hannon, L. *Legal Side of Private Security.* Westport, Conn.: Greenwood Publishing Group, 1992.

Hartsfield, H. *Investigating Employee Conduct.* Deerfield, Ill.: Callaghan & Co., 1988.

Jaspan, Norman. *Mind Your Own Business.* Englewood Cliffs, N.J.: Prentice-Hall, 1974.

Jaspan, Norman and Hillel Black. *The Thief in the White Collar.* Philadelphia: J.B. Lippincott, 1980.

Katzman, G.C. *Inside the Criminal Process.* New York: W.W. Norton, 1991.

Kell, William G., and Robert K. Mautz. *Internal Controls in U.S. Corporations.* New York: Financial Executives Institute Research Foundation, 1980.

Keller, Albert E. *Embezzlement and Internal Control.* Washington, D.C.: Warner-Arms Publishing, 1946.

Kohn, E.J. *Fraud.* New York: Harper & Row, 1973.

Kramer, M.W. *Investigative Techniques in Complex Financial Crimes.* Washington, D.C.: National Institute on Economic Crime, 1989.

Kropatkin, Philip, and Richard P. Kusserow. *Management Principles for Assets Protection: Understanding the Criminal Equation.* New York: John Wiley & Sons, 1986.

Leininger, Sheryl, ed. *Internal Theft: Investigation and Control, an Anthology.* Los Angeles: Security World Publishing, 1975.

Marcella, Albert. *The Hunt for Fraud: Prevention and Detection Techniques.* Altamonte Springs, Fla.: Institute of Internal Auditors, 1994.

Nettler, Gwynn. *Lying, Cheating and Stealing.* Cincinnati: Anderson Publishing, 1982.

Nossen, Richard. *The Determination of Undisclosed Financial Interest.* Washington, D.C.: Government Printing Office, 1979.

Obermaier, H. *White Collar Crime.* New York: Law & Seminars Press, 1990.

Parker, Donn B. *Fighting Computer Crime.* New York: John Wiley & Sons, 1999.

Payne, S. *Art of Asking Questions.* Princeton: Princeton University Press, 1979.

Russell, Harold F. *Foozles and Frauds.* Altamonte Springs, Fla.: Institute of Internal Auditors, 1977.

Snyder, Neil. *Reducing Employee Theft: A Guide to Financial and Organizational Controls.* New York: Quorum Books, 1991.

Somers, L. *Economic Crimes: Investigative Principles and Techniques.* New York: Clark Boardman, 1984.

Thomas, Gordon and Max Morgan-Witts. *The Day the Bubble Burst: A Social History of the Wall Street Crash of 1929.* New York: Doubleday & Co., 1979.

U. S. Sentencing Commission. *Guidelines Manual.* St. Paul, Minn.: West Publishing, 1994.

Villa, J. *Banking Crimes: Fraud, Money Laundering, and Embezzlement.* New York: Clark Boardman, 1988.

Wagner, Charles. *The CPA and Computer Fraud.* Lexington, Mass.: Lexington Books, 1979.

Wales, Stephen H. *Embezzlement and its Control.* Richmond, Ind.: Igelman Publishers, 1965.

Wasik, M. *Crime and the Computer.* Cary, N.C.: Oxford University Press, 1991.

Weisburd, D., S. Wheeler, E. Waring, and N. Bode. *Crimes of the Middle Classes: White-Collar Offenders in the Federal Courts.* New Haven: Yale University Press, 1991.

Wells, Joseph. *Occupational Fraud and Abuse.* Austin, Tex.: Obsidian Publishing, 1997.

Wheeler, S., K. Mann, and A. Sarat. *Sitting in Judgment: The Sentencing of White-Collar Criminals.* New Haven: Yale University Press, 1988.

Williams, Howard. *Investigating Embezzlement and Financial Fraud.* Springfield, Ill.: Charles C. Thomas, 1997.

Zietz, Dorothy. *Women Who Embezzle or Defraud: A Study of Convicted Felons.* New York: Praeger Publishers, 1981.

# Authors' Biographies

Jack Bologna is an associate professor of management at Siena Heights College in Adrian, Michigan, and is the publisher of the monthly newsletters *Forensic Accounting Review* and *Computer Security Digest*. For some 40 years, he has specialized in auditing, investigating, and teaching about white collar crime, and particularly about corporate crimes such as accounting system frauds and embezzlement. He holds degrees in law and accounting and spent 14 years in federal investigative agencies, including the Internal Revenue Service Intelligence Division and the Drug Enforcement Administration. He has authored and coauthored a number of books on these subjects, among them *Accountant's Handbook on Fraud and Commercial Crime; Corporate Fraud: The Basics of Prevention and Detection; Forensic Accounting Handbook, 2nd edition; Fraud Auditing and Forensic Accounting; Fraud Awareness Manual; and Corporate Crime Investigation.*

Paul Shaw is the editor and publisher of *Computing & Communications: Law and Protection and Assets Protection*, the latter periodical covering controls and safeguards to protect company resources. He is the coauthor of the *Fraud Awareness Manual, the Forensic Accounting Handbook*, the *Executive Protection Manual*, and *Corporate Crime Investigation*. He is the author of *Managing Legal and Security Risks in Computing and Communications*.

# *Index*